What Was I Thinking?

What Was I Thinking?
THE DUMB THINGS WE DO
AND HOW TO AVOID THEM

WILLIAM B. HELMREICH, Ph.D.

Taylor Trade publishing

Lanham • New York • Dallas • Boulder • Toronto • Oxford

Published by Taylor Trade Publishing
An imprint of The Rowman & Littlefield Publishing Group, Inc.
4501 Forbes Boulevard, Suite 200, Lanham, Maryland 20706
http://www.rlpgtrade.com

Distributed by NATIONAL BOOK NETWORK

British Library Cataloguing in Publication Information Available

Library of Congress Cataloging-in-Publication Data
Helmreich, William B.
What was I thinking? : the dumb things we do and how to avoid them /
William B. Helmreich.
p. cm.
Includes bibliographical references and index.
ISBN 978-1-58979-597-6 (pbk. : alk. paper) — ISBN 978-1-58979-601-0 (electronic)
1. Errors. 2. Decision making. I. Title.
BF323.E7H45 2011
155.9'2—dc22
2010044192

∞™ The paper used in this publication meets the minimum requirements of American National Standard for Information Sciences—Permanence of Paper for Printed Library Materials, ANSI/NISO Z39.48-1992.

Printed in the United States of America.

contents

To my wife and children

Acknowledgments

$\mathbf{M}$y greatest debt for help in this book is to my wife, Helaine, and to my children, Jeff, Joe, and Deb. They carefully read my manuscript and made literally hundreds of valuable suggestions. They also challenged my assumptions and conclusions, thus refining and expanding my thinking on this endlessly fascinating subject. Jeff, in particular, helped shape and sharpen my ideas with his many thoughtful and perceptive philosophical and legal insights. As an added bonus, my wife and children are all gifted writers in their own rights. Their encouragement, enthusiasm, brilliance, and deep love are always with me.

The following people contributed in many important ways to this book by sharing their insights, thinking, reactions, and resources: First, my agent, John Willig, for his great effort in placing this book and for his infectious optimism. Zach Dicker, Judith Rothman, Ben Sherwood, and Jeff Wiesenfeld did yeoman work in helping me in many ways and have my eternal gratitude. Others who read the manuscript and commented, or who assisted me in other ways, include Arthur and Carole Anderman, Paul Attewell, James Jasper, Mel Berger, Sheldon and Tobie Czapnik, Esther Friedman, Hershey and Linda Friedman, Steve Goldberg, Joan Downs Goldberg, Avery Kotler, Okyun Kwon, Stanley Lupkin, Herbert Rickman, Allan Rudolf,

Charles Sassoon, Arden Smith, David Steinman, and Bill Thomas. I thank them all. Special thanks to the team at Taylor Trade, especially my editor Rick Rinehart, senior production editor Alden Perkins, and copyeditor Erica Nikolaidis.

Introduction

Sports icon Tiger Woods severely damages his reputation in a night of mayhem. He's one of the most famous figures in sports, a multi-millionaire worshiped by legions of adoring fans. Why did he do it?

Bernie Madoff, respected financier, bilks people, many of them his friends, out of millions of dollars. His hubris astounds everyone.

General Stanley McChrystal wrecks his career and is fired by President Barack Obama because of intemperate remarks he made in an interview with *Rolling Stone Magazine*. What made him do it?

Governor Mark Sanford tells people not to disturb him because he's hiking the Appalachian Trail when, in fact, he is consorting with his mistress in Argentina. Did he really think that, as a public figure, he could avoid being found out?

Lisa Nowak, a highly trained and disciplined astronaut, goes ballistic over a failed romance. In a frenzy of rage she drives over nine hundred miles wearing a diaper and threatens her fellow astronaut with an air pistol.

Michael Richards of *Seinfeld* fame destroys his career with a racist tirade that ends up on YouTube. He goes on TV with Reverend Jesse Jackson and defends himself with the "Some of my best friends . . ." argument. No one buys it.

Martha Stewart, an American icon worth hundreds of millions of dollars goes for a paltry $45,000 illegal profit on a stock sale. Her reputation is permanently tarnished.

Former New York chief judge Sol Wachtler becomes obsessed with a woman and ruins his entire career in his efforts to win her back. He initiates a campaign that includes threatening letters and phone calls and ends up doing some hard prison time. What a come-down for a man who'd been a potential governor of his state.

A basketball team loses game after game. The players are listless underachievers. The coach is clearly unable to motivate them and the owner knows it. Yet he doesn't fire the coach. Why?

You sue a plumber over a seventy-five dollar bill. You win in court, but it's a pyrrhic victory, considering all the time you spent on it. Why did you bother?

Someone cuts you off on the highway. Angered, you decide to "teach him a lesson" by tailgating him in a threatening manner. You're so focused on the offending driver that you crash into another car and end up in the hospital. As you lie in bed, you ask yourself, Why did I do that?

You end a long-term friendship over a minor disagreement. As time goes on you come to regret your hasty decision. Why did you do it?

A spur-of-the-moment affair shatters a twenty-five-year marriage, a secure job, and a place in the community. A loss of temper leads to injury, incarceration, or worse. The old life is suddenly gone.

Actor Russell Crowe hurls a telephone at a hotel clerk; Winona Ryder shoplifts; Bill Clinton messes around in a very public place, the White House; Richard Nixon covers up a third-rate burglary; Stephen Ambrose, Pulitzer Prize-winning historian, plagiarizes. And on, and on, and on.

These are the sorts of things that all of us, famous and anonymous, do at one time or another, in countless different ways. We often know we're doing them, yet we seem almost helpless to prevent them from happening. We'll almost always admit they were wrong and that's what's so puzzling.

President Clinton clearly knew the odds of getting caught with Monica Lewinsky were high, and the benefit hardly worth it. How, then, could someone of Clinton's caliber—a Rhodes scholar, a political genius—make a mistake any one of us could have predicted? How could someone so smart have been so dumb?

That's the mystery we will explore, and try to solve, in the pages to come. And it starts by recognizing something important: dumb mistakes involve taking risks that just aren't worth it. When a celebrity shoplifts, the petty gain from one more blouse pales by comparison to the disgrace of the career-ending scandal, if they're caught. Launching a sordid affair in a very public and accessible place is simply foolish—not because you might be caught, but because, as Clinton should have known, it was *obvious* he would be caught. Why, then, do smart people do it anyway, and so often?

Why, then, do some successful people fail, so colossally, in just a few moments of their lives? In this book we'll explore an often overlooked answer to that question. Smart people—or even average people—who do dumb things are not bad calculators. But they have a hidden flaw in their personalities, an *emotional* drive or need they have had, and nursed, all their lives.

An established scholar plagiarizes a few footnotes, or even a key part of his resume, thinking, "It won't catch up with me, because it's just getting me the respect I already deserve." An athlete who sweated for years to make the Major Leagues takes steroids to stay in the game. A person drives recklessly to get to an interview he's worked years to land. It's not that these people don't know that such activities, in general, are dangerous, and not worth the rewards. It's that when it comes to things they think they should have, the risks fade in their minds. This book is an exploration into a universe of human behavior. Its only boundaries are the thoughts, ideas, and actions of human beings.

The focus is on the mistakes they make, the things they say and do to each other that they invariably come to regret. These missteps are described as "dumb" because that is how they are seen by those who commit them and by others.

There is no one answer that explains such behavior. The problem is far too complex and the causes too varied. But we need to begin with society itself. Why? Because there have been profound social changes in the United States over the last fifty years that play a crucial role in how we think and act. Understanding them provides critical answers to how our values have shifted to the point where we can do things that were rarities a half-century ago.

The roots of some of these errors can be found in society, but they are also related to personal deficiencies in human beings. When these two factors combine, the consequences can be and often are devastating. Among the major culprits are deadly sins like arrogance, greed, and an obsession with pride, or honor. They are sins that often overwhelm the common sense that we should be exercising, but somehow cannot. There are also those mistakes that stem from a search for the easy way out of a dilemma, but which actually create even bigger problems.

Others are a consequence of impulses and insecurities that cannot, it seems, be controlled by their initiators. Some of them can be traced to the cornucopia of psychological maladies that afflict millions, problems not serious enough to require hospitalization, but which are disturbing and sufficiently crippling to seriously affect people's lives. And in many instances, people's foolish decisions can be traced to not one, but a number, of interrelated causes.

In this book you will read many tales of human folly. They are told in simple terms. Some of them are amusing, others depressing and even infuriating. They are about the foibles of the powerful, glamorous, and rich—household names like Bill Clinton and George W. Bush, Barry Bonds, Martha Stewart, Britney Spears, Tiger Woods, Don Imus, Eliot Spitzer, Saddam Hussein, Gary Hart, Winona Ryder, and many others. But there are other, equally important stories about the not famous. They are just as significant because they deal with the everyday lives of the hundreds of millions of ordinary mortals who do not make headlines, but who care just as much about happiness and fulfillment.

Yet the purpose here is not simply to tell interesting stories. They have a goal, these anecdotes. Through them, we'll come to understand the *reasons* why people say and do these things. Hundreds of people were interviewed for this book. They include the violators themselves as well as those who know or knew them. They also include the psychiatrists and psychologists who mine the recesses of the human mind in order to uncover and analyze people's insecurities and darkest fears. Lawyers, prosecutors, physicians, businessmen, and just ordinary folks—plumbers, gardeners, homemakers, and salespeople complete our panel of respondents.

To get the right answers you need to ask the right questions. But you also have to let people talk. Just about everyone's got an interesting story to tell; you just need to get them to tell it. I've listened my whole life, and especially for the past five years, as people have described, in emotions ranging from sorrowful to gleeful, the things that have happened to them, the arguments they've had, the disputes in which they were embroiled, the many ways in which they botched an opportunity, how they responded to a crisis, and how they managed to totally mess up their lives.

In these efforts, my training as a sociologist has helped me a great deal. The accounts, involving what could or should have been, shed much light on how, as the song goes, "You Can't Always Get What You Want." The explanations presented further illuminate why we can't or don't. They also show how we are so frequently accomplices in actions that come back to both harm and haunt us.

Reading the stories of the mistakes that people have made will, I firmly believe, offer key insights that can help people avoid similar errors in their own lives. They are cautionary tales and people often absorb knowledge and insight from such accounts that can guide their future behavior. The motivation to learn is, of course, a key factor in making this happen.

The first step toward correcting a mistake is to admit you made one. The second is to understand why you made it. But the third is finding ways to avoid making the mistake again. That is why we offer, in the last chapter, *concrete ideas, approaches, and suggestions*, a road map, if you will, toward preventing missteps in life. These suggestions, while not a cure-all, can go a considerable distance in helping readers increase the satisfaction levels of their lives.

Naturally, people may find it necessary, depending on the problem and its severity, to go for talk therapy, cognitive therapy, and to take medication. But developing insight and understanding, along with willing yourself to follow some simple rules or suggestions, can go a long way.

Since the stories in this book always illustrate and further explain the underlying causes of such behavior—arrogance, insecurity, honor, and so on—they will be equally applicable to new mistakes made by others. And it's highly unlikely that there will ever be a shortage of people doing dumb things. *The names may change but the reasons will not. In that sense, this book is both timely and timeless.* And now, let's begin this exploration with a look at how the world in which we live shapes our understanding of life and our responses when we screw up.

I

THE WORLD WE LIVE IN

We've all done dumb things at some point in our lives, but when they happen to those we admire and sometimes envy for their good fortune, we notice it more. In reality though, these individuals aren't much different from us, or at least they didn't appear that way when they began their lives.

Think of Senator Larry Craig, Bill Clinton, or Tiger Woods as children. Their parents held them in their laps and changed their diapers and they played in the sandbox, just like you and me. They went to school, ate in McDonald's, got into and out of trouble, and were influenced by the world we live in. Britney Spears, Russell Crowe, and Michael Richards all lived in different communities, had ordinary friends growing up, and dreamed, like most of us do, of being rich and famous.

In short, to understand their misdeeds and our own, we need to begin with the society in which we were raised and look at it more closely. And when we do, we'll see how normal events or situations may be directly related to what we do years later, actions that others may condemn as over the top, scandalous, and even crazy.

HOW SOCIETY PLAYS A ROLE IN DUMB BEHAVIOR

People have to take responsibility for their own stupidity. Yet, in many cases they're unable to and society frequently bears a portion of the blame. Here are the main reasons:

1. The particular way in which you were raised
2. The fact that our values are often shaped at a very young age
3. The very real failings of our heroes and icons
4. The failure to accept individual responsibility
5. American society is really many "small societies" and these can support misdeeds of which the larger society strongly disapproves.
6. "Everyone does it."
7. The societal cost of admitting wrongdoing
8. Resenting social pressure to conform
9. The bonds of community are falling apart.
10. We've become a "disposable society."
11. The precipitous drop in the price of scandal

HOW WE WERE RAISED

"Lie down with dogs, get up with fleas," goes the old saying. "You are judged by the company you keep," we are told. And it's true. Sociologists, psychologists, teachers, ministers, all of them believe, correctly, that environment shapes destiny, at least in part. Our values, attitudes, beliefs, and actions are influenced by how we are brought up, who we hang out with, what we see on TV and in the movies, and the music we listen to.

This is not news, of course. We know we are, to some extent, the products of our background and environment. But what seems amazing is that people who transcended their roots in so many ways—

overcame difficult childhoods, outgrew personal handicaps, rose above a narrow outlook, saw things in a new light, dominated mainstream society—could still act in a way that seemed to reflect no awareness of the norms of the world they inhabit.

Psychologists, pundits, and colleagues recoil in shock at how "this well-adjusted person" could have faltered after coming so far. What they fail to notice is that we don't always come so far in our entirety. Parts of our past didn't make the jump with the rest of us, and in the right—or wrong—combination of events, they burst to the surface.

Al Campanis was the respected general manager of the Los Angeles Dodgers, a great job to have and one that makes you think of someone who knows how to deal with people. So it was with amazement and disbelief that viewers watched him self-destruct in a 1987 interview with Ted Koppel on *Nightline*. The program was dedicated to Jackie Robinson, the famous second baseman of the Dodgers, who, in 1946, broke the color line in baseball.

Campanis had been Robinson's teammate and when another player made derogatory comments about Jackie, Al slugged him. This was consistent with Campanis' strong advocacy for blacks throughout his professional career. Midway through the interview, Koppel asked Campanis why so few blacks held senior administrative positions in baseball. After some prodding, in which he denied that discrimination had anything to do with it, Campanis said the most politically incorrect thing someone in his position could say: "I don't believe it's prejudice. I truly believe that they do not have some of the necessities to be, let's say, a field manager, or perhaps, a general manager."

Why, as a media savvy person, would someone like Campanis say something like that even if he believed it? Consider that Campanis grew up in the 1940s, an era when racially charged thinking by whites, even open-minded whites, was very common. It was a time when whites joked about blacks without a trace of self-consciousness. Simply put, Campanis slipped up, but he was stating a view that he had, very likely, held for decades.

Another, more recent case in point is that of Nobel Prize winner James Watson, who in 2007 asserted that, on the whole, blacks were not as smart as whites. Like Campanis, who was forced to resign as general manager, Watson quit as head of the renowned Cold Spring Harbor Laboratory under pressure from his board. And though Watson lives in a different professional world, he is quite similar to Campanis in terms of age and background.

Don Imus is a twofer. Like Campanis and Watson, he's from that earlier period in American history when you could get away with stuff like that. But he also belongs to another group not known for its attention to propriety—the shock-jock culture. And, in truth, Imus had been getting away with it for years. The only difference was that this time he crossed too many lines at once. In making crude and racist comments about Rutgers University players, he knocked young black women who had fought their way out of the inner city, who had risen to stardom on one of the best teams in the country, who were attending a good university, and who were, by their actions, making Imus look like a relic of the past who had no class, especially after they readily accepted his belated apology.

A year later, all seemed forgiven, as Jesse Jackson's early denunciations lapsed into silence and as another vocal critic, Al Sharpton, observed that Imus "has not been offensive" since then. "We were not trying to destroy Imus," he said. "I hope he does well."

Researchers have proven how strong an impact culture has on people. In a famous experiment, Stanford University professor Philip Zimbardo showed that almost anyone can cross the line between good and evil. College students were divided into groups of prisoners and of guards and placed in a fake jail. The change from regular guys to vicious, sadistic guards was so quick that the experiment had to be abandoned within a week.

Even the participants reported being appalled that they could become so cruel to people they didn't know and had nothing against. In follow-up interviews, Zimbardo discovered little, if any difference between various personality types and how likely they were to be nasty to others. Rather, it was the situation that determined their actions.

Zimbardo overstates the case a bit. The situation can and does exercise a powerful influence, but we're not all cut from the same cloth. If we were, people wouldn't be so different from each other in their personalities, attitudes, behaviors, and abilities. People have varied responses to danger, illness, jokes, music, other people, and just about everything.

Still, if something is happening and it's very intense, people can get caught up, especially when they're with others, and act out of character. Suppose you are caught up in a desire to avenge a wrong. Someone has physically thrown your close friend out of a party for no apparent reason. A crowd gathers. Everyone's excited. You decide to take action by attacking the host and you wind up in jail. Were you more apt, because of your Type A personality, to act? Possibly, but had you not been part of the crowd, you probably would not have done so.

STARTING YOUNG

My cousin is a born teacher. Tall, thin, and wiry, with crystal blue eyes and a thinning shock of blonde hair, he's an intense fellow who takes what he does very seriously. Tim* went into teaching because he really believes in it. He has fully bought into the idea that he can change young people's lives for the better and he isn't close to burning out.

One day, while we were having a quiet lunch, a parent of one of his students walked into the restaurant and, spotting Tim, came over and said hello. "This is Dr. Rawick," my cousin said, introducing him to me. After exchanging some pleasantries, the man moved on. "You know," Tim said, "It's really amazing. This guy teaches medical ethics

---

*Names and minor details in some of the stories have been changed to protect the privacy of individuals.

at the university and his son is involved in a major cheating scandal in our high school. In fact, he's one of the ringleaders."

"So what's new," I replied, with a laugh. "Cheating's been with us forever. And I'll admit it's more aggravating when someone like that, whose father teaches ethics, does it. But my question to you is, why is it so widespread when everybody agrees in principle that it's wrong?"

"I'm not really sure," my cousin said, "but I'll tell you one thing. It doesn't start in high school." Leaning forward in his chair, the way he usually does when something is really bothering him, he looked intently at me, and continued. "When a parent entering the subway tells his kid, who's six years old and has to pay the fare, to tell the token booth guy that he's five so that he can ride free, that's when it starts. By the time he gets to high school, it's too late."

Tim was absolutely right, I've concluded. As everyone knows, our kids know the truth. They know when we're sermonizing, when we're sincere, and when we're being hypocritical. And they don't hesitate to throw it up to us just when we least expect it or want to hear it. A study done by Public Agenda, a New York-based research outfit, reports that, while a high percentage of parents object to their children copying other kids' homework, many see nothing wrong with doing their own child's homework assignments. In other words, it's okay as long as you keep it in the family. And so another chance to teach a moral lesson is lost.

Small wonder then, that cheating is rampant in our schools. Professor Donald McCabe of Rutgers University is an expert on cheating. In surveys of fourteen thousand college students between 2006 and 2010 he found that 40 percent admitted to having cheated on exams and assignments. And that's only those who confessed to it. At MIT, 20 percent of the students were found, in one study, to have copied one-third or more of their homework.

Our message, in so many ways, has been that it's okay. This kind of wink-and-look-the-other-way attitude creates a snowball effect. As more and more people do it, it encourages even greater numbers to participate. Many of these are students with moral qualms about cheating. But they are resentful that others get away with it and then reap the rewards of higher grades when they apply to law school or for a job.

What this all adds up to is that we have been nurtured in and live in a cheating culture. Of course, it's been with us for a long time. Think of the Robber Barons and all of the financial scandals that were widespread a century ago. But when Charles Van Doren was caught cheating on a quiz show in 1957, it was a scandal. Today, it would probably not be as shocking. In the back of our minds most of us believe that such shows are generally fixed. In fact, most evidence suggests that the number of cheaters is going up. A 2002 study of twelve thousand high school students discovered that 74 percent of them said they'd cheated on an exam at least once in the previous year, up from 61 percent in a 1992 survey.

FAILINGS OF THE RICH AND FAMOUS

Yet, we haven't totally lost our ability to be shocked. When Doris Kearns Goodwin, one of our most highly regarded historians, was accused of plagiarism (ironically, she's the wife of the author, Richard Goodwin, who chronicled the "Quiz Show Scandal," and who prosecuted the producers), many were dismayed. Ditto for Stephen Ambrose, another historian regarded as a first-rate scholar. And in both cases, the plagiarism charges came *after* they'd won the Pulitzer Prize. Why did they do it? Hadn't they already reached the pinnacle of success? One reason was that they were really a reflection of the culture in which they and we live and which, ironically, they wrote about. And so, what seems out of character may, in a sense, not really be so at all. It's as if we held up a mirror and, instead of seeing ourselves, saw our role models, tarnished and all too human.

Historians are apparently not the only ones accused of plagiarism. Jessica and Jerry Seinfeld were sued by Missy Chase Lapine, who accused Jessica of "brazen plagiarism," asserting that she lifted material in her book, *Deceptively Delicious*, from Lapine's work, *The Sneaky Chef*. In response to these accusations of sneaky behavior, Jerry called Lapine "a wacko" and said, in his own inimitable style, that "if you read history, many of the three-name people do become assassins." (I guess that means John Wilkes Booth, Lee Harvey Oswald and James Earl Ray, but not Ralph Waldo Emerson and Billy Jean King!) The lawsuit was dismissed by a federal appeals court in April 2010.

Acceptance of cutting corners and much, much more, is nowhere more widespread than in the world of business. Haven't Enron, BP, and Toyota, become synonyms for irresponsibility, corruption, and cover-ups? Hardly a day goes by without some financial bigwig accused or convicted of some wrongdoing. The Martha Stewart case was widely discussed and dominated the news for months, but not because of what she did. After all, probably thousands of people benefit from insider information, most often referred to as "tips," when buying and selling stocks.

No, the issue was *who* Martha Stewart was. She was a cultural hero, a role model who advised us on how to behave and on what to do in our homes. A fashion model, stockbroker par excellence, prolific author, and TV hostess of her own show—one watched by millions—she seemed to have it all. And if she could fall, then anyone could. And yet, what most people actually concluded was that she was targeted as both an example and a scapegoat because of her fame and power, while most people who did what she did continued to get away with it.

What Stewart, Ambrose, and Kearns Goodwin all had in common was that they were so successful that their "crimes" didn't make sense to most of us. They appeared to be totally unnecessary. To really get a handle on that question we have to look to psychology and psychiatry. The reasons are varied and complex, but there is no doubt that our culture plays a major role.

After all, who is Martha Stewart? A native of Jersey City, New Jersey, Martha Helen Kostyra was one of six children raised in a middle class Polish-American family. Bright, ambitious, and hardworking, she went to Barnard College, married, and had a child. Her personal life was unexceptional, but what set her apart was the degree to which she succeeded. Self made, she was seen as a true Horatio Alger prototype, named in 2004 by *Ladies Home Journal* as "the third most powerful woman in America."

Stewart was worth hundreds of millions of dollars when she was charged in 2001 with selling 3,928 shares of her ImClone stock. She saved herself $45,673, a paltry, meaningless sum given her tremendous wealth. Let's remember, however, that in the business circles in which she and many others travel, gaining from a stock tip was pretty routine.

WHO'S RESPONSIBLE?

And what about the responsibility of the individual? The argument that we are products of our society bothers many people. To them it means that every time we do something wrong, we can just blame it on someone else. In one sensational case that occurred in 2001, thirteen-year-old Lionel Tate was convicted in Fort Lauderdale of stomping and beating a six-year-old girl to death. In what can only be described as colossal chutzpah, his lawyers claimed that Tate was imitating professional wrestling moves he'd seen on TV!

Of course, this is an extreme case, but it makes the point very well. Don't lawyers often argue that a criminal grew up in a broken home, lived in a neighborhood where violence was a daily feature of life, and suffered abuse from a brother, an uncle, or someone else? And if society is a main culprit, then punishing someone is morally wrong.

These arguments clash head on, however, with a hallowed concept in American culture, namely individualism. Free choice and taking responsibility for one's actions run deeply through the fabric of our society. Ministers tell their congregants that they have the power, with the help, of course, of God, to save themselves. A flood of self-help books have been penned over the years, telling us how we can and should take control of our lives, that it's up to us to do it.

As is so often the case when issues are debated, both sides have a point. We are, in many ways, accountable for what we do. But in almost everything we do, we are influenced by what's going on around us and by so many things that have happened to us in the past. The debate lies in how much weight to give to each.

THE "SMALL SOCIETIES"

While there is something called American culture, the term is somewhat misleading and inaccurate. Our society is really made up of many different groups that have their own value systems, attitudes, and customs. As examples we have Hispanic-Americans, skiers, born-again Christians, stamp collectors, gang members, senior citizens, New Yorkers, and so on. Sociologists call these distinct groups *subcultures.* In some ways they are similar to Americans in general; in others they are unique.

When confronted with outrageous bloopers by famous people, psychologists and journalists often rush in to explain how the hero's losing his or her grip. Did Campanis have a breakdown? Did Imus suddenly burst out with an eruption of hostility long simmering in his subconscious? Was it family troubles?

All of the above do, and have, happened, but what these explanations miss is that there may have been no break at all. In some of these public mistakes, the individual may not have acted out of character. Rather, his or her character acted out—escaped the bounds of his or her later life and returned to the ways that shaped him or her. We all break into the mainstream culture from another domain— our subculture, a little cocoon we don't highlight on our resumes or thank in award ceremonies, but which is very much a part of us.

And all too often, that subculture teaches us what to do in a way that clashes with the demands of the larger culture, the one we find ourselves inhabiting—and being confronted by when we go astray.

Let's look at football superstar Michael Vick. His crime, killing dogs and supporting a dog-fighting operation, Bad Newz Kennels, was not something supported or even tolerated by the average American. The consequences were very serious—real jail-time, a lucrative career in jeopardy, and a whole slew of product endorsements that went up in smoke.

Dog fighting has been traced all the way back to the Roman Empire and was common in medieval England. In recent years it has been popular among poor blacks, Hispanics, and whites, especially in parts of the deep South. Vick grew up in this environment and it was one where the sport, however odious, was not seen as "a real crime." This, no doubt, figured in his attitude towards it. That doesn't excuse his cruelty to animals, but it does help explain it.

Members of a subculture often see nothing terrible with what they're doing and are shocked when others view it as very wrong. We have no better example of this than Watergate. Paranoia about the Democrats had become a part of the Nixon White House culture. As a result, the administration approved breaking and entering and wiretapping without any compunction, even though, in the larger society, such acts were perceived as clearly illegal, which they were. Had those involved in what was widely called "a third-rate burglary" talked to people beyond their closed circle, the response just might have prevented the whole thing from happening. We'll never know.

The possible implications of such isolation were brought home when NBC TV hired me as a consultant not long after my book on the truth and origins of stereotypes, *The Things They Say Behind Your Back*, came out. They wanted to evaluate their TV shows with respect to how, where, and when racial and ethnic stereotypes could be most acceptably and effectively employed. For example, at what point would the lines, from funny, to insensitive, to outright bigotry, be crossed?

On one occasion, we gathered in Laguna Niguel, California, and spent a few days in a hotel reviewing the shows and the material. The legendary Brandon Tartikoff, who headed NBC's entertainment division, warned me that the writers for the shows "lived in their own world." He was absolutely right. They were writing shows that would be seen by millions of viewers—*Miami Vice*, *The Cosby Show*, *Hill Street Blues*—and yet they seemed curiously removed from the rest of the world. As creative people, they functioned in almost an enclosed bubble, hanging out, for the most part, with each other.

The effects of this became clear to me from the way they approached the problem before them. One of the writers said to me, "So, we just use this list of stereotypes and not the other?" There was no thought of debating which ones were appropriate, which weren't, and why, just a question of being told what to do. Brandon was very different, far more worldly, and he cautioned me that the writers probably needed to get out more often and "hang with ordinary folks."

This was an easily correctible situation, but often it's not, and when that happens, the consequences can be serious. When Ronald Reagan went to Bitburg, Germany, in 1985 to lay a wreath at a cemetery where forty-nine members of the Waffen-SS were buried, he did not realize how this offended Jews around the world. The Nobel Laureate, Elie Wiesel, pointedly said to him "That place is not your place."

But Reagan just didn't get it, despite the fact that he considered himself, and in fact was, a good friend of the Jewish community. This was demonstrated when he defended himself by saying that most of the two thousand men buried there "were victims of Nazism." He was then accused of equating German soldiers who fought against the Allies with victims of Nazi death camps. So we see that the rarefied atmosphere of the White House can occasionally insulate even the savviest of politicians. To commemorate the PR disaster, the rock group, The Ramones, recorded the song, "My Brain is Hanging Upside Down—Bonzo Goes to Bitburg."

Or let's take plagiarism and even outright fabrication, both of which have been coming under increasing scrutiny in recent years, hitting some of the most venerable and well-known news organs such as the *New York Times*, *USA Today*, and the *New Republic*. Various villains have been identified—pressure to do stories, the need to fill space, lack of proper supervision.

What has also been revealed through books by Jayson Blair, formerly of the *Times*, and Stephen Glass, who wrote for the *New Republic*, is that there are staffers within these organizations who are aware of and tolerate it, creating a little subculture whose members look the other way when they know they shouldn't. The *New Republic* ran some twenty-five pieces by Glass containing questionable information, a number of which could correctly be classified as fiction. Shockingly, the magazine said, "We offer no excuses. Only apologies."

Then there's the case of John White, a black man who came from a community where certain fears and apprehensions predominated. These emotions were cited by the lawyers who defended him when he was charged with murder. White confronted a group of white teenagers who stood on his lawn in Miller Place, Long Island, shouted racial slurs, and threatened him.

White claimed that he feared for his life and invoked his family history in support of his statement. His grandfather had been run out of Alabama in the 1920s by the Ku Klux Klan. As a result, when he found himself facing angry whites and the glare of car headlights, it reminded him of the lynch mobs that had attacked blacks in the deep South. He had a gun in his hand to protect himself and he either fired it at Daniel Cicciaro or it went off accidentally, depending on whom you believe. Whatever the case, a young man lay dead as a result of an uncharacteristic response by a clearly frightened man who raised the specter of history and culture in his defense.

John White, a construction foreman, had an unblemished record. He had never been arrested or convicted of anything before that night.

The house he had bought was in a mostly white neighborhood and represented his version of "The American Dream." As that dream shattered into a thousand pieces on a sweltering August evening in 2006, White turned to his wife and said: "We lost the house. We lost it all." Indeed he had. White was convicted of second-degree manslaughter.

"EVERYONE DOES IT"

"Everyone does it," was one of the most common refrains I heard in the hundreds of interviews conducted for this book. Here's what a typical businessman had to say about this and other illegal, or at least, questionable practices:

> Ninety-nine percent of crooked behavior has to do with our society. And it's like that all over the world. One of my European business associates tells me that there's a line on the expense accounts of people like him who do business with other countries. It's called bribes! I have another friend who built, like, 50,000 square feet for Nike. He's built stuff for Kohl, The Limited, lots of huge companies. He has a great personality. He takes these people to dinner and they laugh from beginning to end. He takes them to expensive hotels, rents limos for them, and gets them Super Bowl tickets. Everybody's doing it and so he has to. In the end though, the bottom line isn't how smart you are, how funny you are. It's what's in it for the person. And the proportion of people who get caught is so tiny.

What comes through here, loud and clear, is a deep cynicism about our system, but coupled with an acceptance that this is life and anyone who doesn't think so is just naive. Similarly, when we hear about all the Wall Street executives who knew that the subprime market was a ticking time bomb, one that would cause financial ruin for perhaps millions of people, we are upset. We express outrage that these individuals made millions from the misfortunes of the proverbial little guy, but at some level, we are not surprised. Sure, we know that some big shots, people like Tyco's Dennis Koslowski, WorldCom's Bernard Ebbers, and Enron's Jeffrey Skilling, have been punished. Their convictions will, in certain circles, be presented as evidence that the system works. In reality, the number of such convictions, compared to the amount of violators still out there, is but a drop in the bucket and everyone knows it.

"Everyone does it" is often the fallback option when people cannot otherwise justify their behavior. In May 2003, Rick Bragg, a Pulitzer-Prize winning reporter, resigned from the *New York Times* amid charges that he had written an article about Florida Gulf Coast oystermen whom he had never interviewed and that he had depended primarily on the work of a freelance journalist for his information. Speaking in his own defense, Bragg asserted that, "most national correspondents will tell you they rely on stringers and researchers and interns and clerks and news assistants." This accusation was then followed by heated denials from other journalists.

We've all been told that just because others do something doesn't make it right, but the power of numbers does make it *seem* right to many people, even if they admit that it isn't. When crimes occur and people are asked why they didn't step in, they frequently say, "No one else did anything either."

Former president Bill Clinton was surely aware that he was not the first holder of the office to have fooled around. Grover Cleveland paid child support for an out-of-wedlock child. Franklin Delano Roosevelt had an affair with Lucy Page Mercer, his wife's social secretary. Ike Eisenhower reportedly had an affair with Kay Summersby. As for Kennedy and Johnson, they were each widely rumored to have had numerous affairs.

What all this means is that Clinton, in looking at past presidential history, had good reason to assume that Americans would tolerate his errant behavior with a "What do you expect?" response, along with observations that such affairs involving men of affairs are not even much remarked upon in the Middle East, Europe, and Latin America, in short, everywhere except, maybe, the U.S. That it was, truly surprised him.

The belief by people that "everyone does it," is a dangerous perception. If not challenged and refuted, it can have real consequences. This is because it will embolden people who might otherwise see wrongdoing as unacceptable to actually cross the line and engage in it.

In truth, many people have already crossed that line because they've seen other "respected" individuals doing it. When Joe Average reads a story about a doctor who routinely overbilled patients or who performed unnecessary operations, what is he supposed to think? Here's a man, a doctor no less, making more money than he'll ever see and he has the nerve to overcharge.

A student is scolded by her professor for not citing sources in her term paper, but she has just seen a report on TV about scientific researchers who faked data. "Why should I be held to a higher standard?" she thinks. Is it surprising when she concludes that her only crime was in getting caught?

I know of a case where young men and women working as interviewers for a research project took the questionnaires they were supposed to administer to others, went to the beach, and filled them out themselves while lying in the sun. And why not? After all, they reasoned, journalists can write stories about places they've never seen and get them published. Then, when they're exposed, they claim, without shame, that the practice is "routine."

Think about it. Athletes in this country are among the most disciplined people in the world. They are the role models for millions of young Americans. Their success is both hoped for and sought after. The path leading to it can only be reached by hard work, constant practice, and, of course, talent. And then, the story of Barry Bonds explodes into the media. A baseball superstar is charged with having used steroids repeatedly for years. He's a cheat and a crook.

We also read about former Olympian runner Marion Jones, similarly charged with steroid use. Papers filed by her lawyers seeking probation for the convicted superstar said, "She has been cast from American hero to national disgrace. The public scorn, from a nation that once adored her, and her fall from grace, have been severe punishments."

But these are exceptions, we are told, or want to be told. Who wants to watch sports and find out it's fixed or dishonest? Remember the 1919 Chicago White Sox? Eight team members were convicted of trying to throw the World Series and that team became infamous as the Chicago Black Sox. And when the culprits are punished we breathe a sigh of relief, especially the coaches, recruiters, university presidents, and professional team owners for whom sports is big business, not to mention the builders and operators of stadiums and sports equipment manufacturers. We need our heroes and they need us.

That's why we're quick to forgive Tiger Woods. All he has to do is issue a sincere-sounding apology. And then, before you know it, he's back on the golf tour circuit.

What were Barry Bonds and Marion Jones thinking? we ask ourselves. Did they really believe they could get away with it? So why did they do it? Weren't they talented enough without these performance enhancers? And now they know they must pay the price, we say to ourselves. Alas, it's not that simple.

On December 13, 2007, all hell broke loose in organized sports. That was the day former senator George Mitchell released an historic report that named eighty-nine baseball players as steroid users. The list included many marquee players, All Stars like Roger Clemens, Andy Pettitte, Gary Sheffield, Jose Canseco, and Mo Vaughn.

More shocking than these names, perhaps, was the extent of their steroid use. Many correctly assumed, it appears, that the eighty-nine players represented only those known to the commission, and that there were others. Was doping the norm in sports? And if so, what could and should be done? The only beneficiary perhaps, was Barry Bonds. It now seemed that he had a lot of company.

The response was delivered by none other than the senator himself, who recommended that the players not be punished. "This was a collective failure to recognize the problem as it emerged and to deal with it early on. . . . Everybody in baseball—commissioners, club officials, the players' association—shares responsibility."

Was there really a choice? One can make examples of two or three people, but an entire profession? One hundred or more players? Mitchell laid the blame precisely where it belonged—on a culture that had refused to face the problem, that tolerated and encouraged such behavior by doing nothing, except maybe making a scapegoat out of Barry Bonds, a sourpuss whose glare and nasty demeanor had become as famous as his dope-enhanced and now-tainted home runs. And now we know what Bonds and others, like Roger Clemens of "misremembering" fame, were thinking. Why would anything happen to me? Am I the only one taking steroids?

THE DOWNSIDE OF ADMITTING WRONGDOING

As if the pervasiveness of such malfeasance wasn't enough to encourage it, there's another problem. The very painful fallout often makes people reluctant to uncover it even if they agree it's wrong. When a scandal is exposed the financial losses can be huge. Ballplayers involved in the scandal will now be less marketable as players, and their agents will suffer similarly. Wall Street firms associated with financial improprieties will see their business affected as investors lose confidence in them. Hospitals charged with improper care lose patients. How many people in baseball now wish they'd never seen the Mitchell Report, or even asked for an investigation?

The pressure to protect vested interests sometimes influences the very people who are supposed to set the standard for what's right and what's wrong. Bob Waters is the principal of a fancy private school in California. In his late forties, Waters exudes both confidence and competence. I asked him about how schools teach values. "It starts in the home, to be honest," he says, "and our job is to nurture and improve on it." He waxes enthusiastic about the number of his students accepted to elite colleges, about the community service programs, and about how genuinely nice the students are.

"What about cheating? I mean, even the best schools have it."

"I'd be lying if I said we didn't," he responds. "And we don't condone it."

"But what do you do about it, actually?" I press.

Waters shifts uncomfortably in his chair. He looks out the window of his office and is silent for almost a full minute before responding. "I'll tell you something which you probably won't hear from other administrators, but I want you to see the problem, from my perspective, from the school's perspective.

"I don't know what percentage of the students in my school cheat, but if you catch someone it's a real pain in the butt. It becomes a whole rigmarole. You have to call in the parents, the kid, of course. There are meetings with teachers, the guidance department gets involved. At the end of the day, it's actually much easier to put on blinders."

"But isn't dealing with such behavior the school's responsibility?" I ask.

Waters adjusts his tie and folds his arms, almost assuming a defensive posture. He has stopped smiling. "What do you think we are, detectives? Spies?" he asks rhetorically. "I'm trained to be an educator, an institutional leader, not a cop. There's just so much we can do. This is a general problem in our culture." His voice rising slightly, he continues. "These kids' parents are all cheating on their income taxes. Do restaurant waiters and cab drivers report their tips? Lawyers lie and get big bucks to do so. Spokesmen for CEOs lie. The president's spokesman lies."

"I understand that. You're right," I say. "But still, isn't the school one of the places where we're supposed to teach people that these things are wrong? And what about the school's reputation? Wouldn't it harm your high school's reputation if word gets around that you tolerate cheating, that you don't do anything about it? I don't just mean your school. I mean any school."

"That's where you're wrong," Waters snaps impatiently. "Totally wrong. What will harm our reputation is if there's a public scandal, if it gets out. Believe me, the parents don't want to know about it. Frankly, my job is to contain the scandal, to deal with it effectively, but quietly. Because if the colleges hear that there's a massive cheating scandal, it'll affect our admissions rate. And then the parents will get mad, especially if their own kids are involved. Not at the kids, but at us, for telling them and messing up their kids' chances to get into a good college. And if everybody gets mad enough, then the whole school will go down the tubes. And that's reality, my friend."

The interview was over. I thanked him and we shook hands. I knew I would remember the conversation as a defining moment in my search for answers as to why people act out of character, if indeed they do. As I walked out of the building, I saw a couple of students lying on the grass in the shade of a large maple tree, reading. Others nearby were playing Frisbee. It was a beautiful, sun-drenched, California day. How bucolic, I thought wistfully. It would make a nice picture in an ad for the school. But it surely wouldn't tell the whole story. Not even close.

RESENTING CONFORMITY

One of the common threads running through many of these stories is peer pressure. While the coach cannot use this as an explanation, his players can. High jinks at school, be it sex in frat houses or getting drunk, are considered almost rites-of-passage, not only for football players, but for students in general. Those who don't go along are often seen as nerds and squares and who wants that?

We've all heard about the "blue wall of silence," or how the police close ranks when one of their own is accused of corruption. Other professions have a similar, "it's us against the world" attitude. "Nobody likes a rat," they say and one can therefore understand, without condoning it, why, for example, newspaper reporters would be hesitant about turning in their own. For some, it's only a short distance to the next step, actually engaging in plagiarism, as a way of expressing approval of such actions.

But there are also times when people do something that's dumb simply in reaction to the pressures of having to conform to what society expects of them. We may resent having to kowtow to others, having to dress a certain way, say the right things, worry about hurting the feelings of others, having to get up early, to work long hours, in short, all the things that people need to do but don't feel like doing.

The cult movie, *Office Space*, exemplified that attitude in the extreme. In it, the main character decides one day that he won't go to work until and unless he feels like it and that he won't do what his boss tells him because he's simply tired of taking crap from everybody at a job that he really doesn't like. In the movie, through a series of twists of fate, he gets away with it, but, as we know, in real life, you don't get away with it. Instead, you're fired.

Sometimes, this sense of always having to do the right thing, the smart thing, the prudent thing, can really lead us astray to the point where we rebel and do something really foolish and then kick ourselves for having been so stupid. Have you ever wondered why people who seem bright, who should have known better allow themselves to be duped by all sorts of pretty obvious scams and schemes— Nigerian investment deals, phony land offers, British lottery jackpots that they haven't won, and the like? It turns out that more than one in ten Americans (mostly elderly but, by no means senile) succumb to such frauds annually.

Another, even more important reason why we feel a need to "break out" from society's rules is because we live in a society where we often feel, correctly, that we don't matter much as individuals, that we can't have any meaningful impact on society. And we want to. That probably explains why people wave to the camera when they're accidentally filmed in the course of a live news story, or why they hold up ridiculous signs at public events. Occasionally, we do something nutty in the hopes of getting some attention. It's a natural impulse, a way of showing that we count. And, once in a while, we pull a crazy prank just for the hell of it, go too far, and get into real trouble.

THE BONDS OF COMMUNITY ARE FALLING APART

In a much-discussed and, ultimately disturbing book published in 2000, *Bowling Alone*, Harvard sociologist Robert Putnam told us something that we probably already suspected. The social fabric that held us together as a community was beginning to fray, perhaps even crumble. We were no longer joining and participating in groups, clubs, or organizations as we had in the past. PTA membership was down, church participation was declining anywhere from 25 to 50 percent, depending on how you calculated it.

But more than that, we simply were hanging out less with one another. People were not meeting on the corner in their neighborhoods, they weren't going as often to bars and nightclubs or to the movies, choosing instead to stay home and "veg out." Putnam produced reams of statistics to make his point, along with striking examples. Take bowling. Through the years there was a profound shift in *how* people bowled. Starting in the 1980s, league bowling decreased by more than 40 percent. I know. I'm a small part of that decrease.

In 1973, I began teaching at City College of New York and lived in an apartment in Forest Hills, Queens. There was a bowling alley two blocks away called Hollywood Lanes. I signed up for one of the leagues. It was for *Daily News* employees, but outsiders could join. I met people, engaged in the easy banter that bowlers everywhere participate in while waiting for their thirty seconds of actual bowling when it's their turn, ate and drank, and generally had a lot of fun. I didn't know anyone at first, but was made to feel welcome.

In December 2007, thirty-five years later, I walked into a bowling alley in northern Queens late one afternoon to see what was happening. I teach a course on the sociology of New York City at CUNY Graduate Center and as part of the preparation time, I regularly walk through the city's neighborhoods, exploring, scoping out interesting places to take my students on our weekly walking tours. It was early on a Tuesday evening and what I found kind of shocked me. There was hardly anyone there. Five of the fifteen lanes were in use. The others were eerily silent, the pins seemingly waiting in the darkness for the joyous, crashing noise that signals a strike.

On three of the lanes in use, pairs of men in perhaps their sixties or early seventies bowled in almost rote fashion. One, a pudgy, bald man with a beer belly, wore a sleeveless undershirt; the other wore a tee shirt with a few small holes in it and a Yankee baseball cap from which a few strands of white hair protruded over a wrinkled forehead. Their deliberate movements as they threw the ball and their failure to react to the result conveyed a certain lack of enthusiasm, even boredom.

Middle-aged men occupied the other two lanes. You knew they were serious from the black gloves they wore and the gleaming green balls they used, not the scuffed and chipped cheapo balls supplied by the alley. They were regulars and they were good. But they were, in fact, bowling alone.

I walked over to the shoe rental counter. A dour-faced man in a plaid flannel shirt and black Dockers sat on a worn leather swivel chair, idly flipping through an auto-racing magazine. "Yeah, whadda ya want?" he asked in a slightly annoyed tone of voice, as if I had just interrupted him in the middle of a nap.

"Do you still have leagues?"

"We have 'em on the weekends."

"As much as in the past?"

"Nah. When I was growing up in the sixties and seventies, you always had people coming around lookin' for the action. There's definitely been a decline over the years in general and with the leagues. Alleys have been closing all over the city, in the Bronx, Brooklyn, and Queens. We've had to diversify so now we have a catering hall too. But I'm hopin' for a resurgence."

The changes are everywhere, Putnam tells us. The NAACP, the Rotary and Elks clubs have all seen big drops in membership. Bridge clubs are breaking up, he wrote, and family circles are having more trouble getting together. This last development is also something I know from personal experience. Members of our own family circle got together far more often twenty years ago than they do today. When they do, usually at my urging, they exclaim, "This is so much fun. We should do it more often." But they don't. Nor, from my anecdotal knowledge, do many other families I know.

Many reasons have been given for this turn of events. The family is breaking down, we have less time, suburbanization means increased commuting time, there are generational changes, and much more. Whatever the cause, the overall result is unmistakable. We are becoming disconnected from our coworkers, friends, family, neighbors, and people in general.

Much has been made about the Internet's impact on our social lives. But does it facilitate or hinder communication? As James Katz and Ronald Rice argue in their important book, *Social Consequences of Internet Use*, the Internet allows people to instantly communicate their feelings, thus preventing the buildup of tension. Moreover, for those uncomfortable with relating to people directly, it's less stressful.

But there's also a downside. The face-to-face interaction so important to social life is missing from the Internet. Without that, an important tool for understanding what people really mean is lost. When we see someone in the flesh, we can observe anger, happiness, sadness, doubt, gratitude, and love; in short, all the emotions that enable us to decide what to do.

Why is all this so important for our question of why people do dumb things? Because people who function alone are more likely to do things that are not smart or good. When we don't have sustained contact with other people, the social bonds that connect us are loosened. And once that happens we become less interested in and dependent on what others think.

The more we interact with others, the smaller the chances that we will do something that we only see as irresponsible or foolish after the damage has been done and it's too late. Connecting with others gives us the opportunity to test out our views, to see if our opinions, and even intentions, are "off the wall." A friend may say, "That's really dumb. You'll be sorry," or "Are you kidding? You'll never get away with that. Calm down!" Without such encounters, people are far more apt to give in to their darkest desires and worst impulses. With them, angry or frustrated people, and aren't we all at times, can be placated or disarmed through understanding and compassion.

But doesn't less group involvement hold out the possibility that we might also be less involved with "bad groups" whose members might encourage us to behave badly? Not nearly as likely, because the norm in society is to conform. Most of us are law-abiding, not out of fear, but because we've bought into it. Therefore, when people get together, it's usually the good, not the bad, that is reinforced. Society fosters norms of cooperation and altruism because if it didn't, it couldn't survive and thrive. Putnam concludes that in America, "those of us who belong to formal and informal social networks are more likely to give our time and money to good causes than those of us who are isolated socially."

But isn't it the larger culture that has given rise to the almost cult-like worship of success? Wouldn't we still be better off withdrawing? Even if we would, we simply can't do it. Man is and has always been a basically social animal. What we need to do is to work on ways to change and improve the world we live in even as we remain in it.

One cautionary note before we accept this thesis uncritically. It isn't just a question of belonging. It's the nature of your belonging.

People can look like they belong when, in fact, nothing could be further from the truth. The Virginia Tech mass murderer, Seung Hui Cho, was in a college dorm suite, belonged to a family, and attended a small English class. But to all of those groups, he was what Princeton professor Katherine Newman, an authority on school shootings, would call, "a failed joiner."

THE DISPOSABLE SOCIETY

There's another huge downside to technology: it has turned us into a disposable society. If your computer breaks, you get another one. The same holds true for your cell phone or TV. Nobody fixes anything anymore. And when they do, like your car mechanic, they simply replace parts, as opposed to repairing them.

This has changed how we think about things in general and that includes how we relate to each other. Take marriage. The divorce rate today is so high in part because people are far less willing to work through their problems. You have a fight with your spouse, that's it. You decide this isn't going to work and you end it. Sometimes it's the right move, but many times it's a major mistake. We're sorry, but it's too late. Or, like that perfectly good kitchen you replaced with a new one, you just got tired of your wife or husband and married someone younger. Five years later, he or she dumps you and you feel the pain so deeply, you want to kill yourself. But again, it's too late to go back.

In the never-ending quest for happiness we often raise our expectations to unrealistic levels. We're looking for "something special." In their book, *A Generation at Risk: Growing Up in an Era of Family Upheaval*, Paul Amato and Alan Booth found that 70 percent of divorces involved low-conflict situations. These failed marriages lacked real marital strife, with three quarters of respondents saying they rarely argued and didn't disagree on much of anything. Parallel to this, the demands of singles have risen. A recent study by the National Marriage

Project reported that a high percentage of singles insist that marriage must be to a "soul mate." Demands of this sort bring to mind the adage, "The perfect is the enemy of the good."

Technology has affected us in yet another way that impacts our human relationships. The constant bombardment of stimuli—radios, TVs, iPods, cell phones, computers, and Blackberries in constant use—has forced us to learn how to multitask. It's an important and necessary skill in today's times, but the ability to do so has come at a high social price, for we have also lost much of our ability to focus.

What this means is that we suffer from MADD—mass attention deficit disorder. The word *patience* is fast becoming an anachronism. When our computer doesn't download something in ten seconds we become frustrated. When there's a commercial on TV during a football game, we flip through twenty channels, rather than just relaxing for a minute.

The insistence on immediate gratification has become part of our general outlook on life. When we were kids, our parents or teachers were fond of saying "haste makes waste." How many products of our technological society today would say that? This can and often does damage us personally, because if we can't or won't take the necessary time to work on our relationships, then we can't resolve the issues that lead to their breakdown. More often than not, the outcome is a rash decision that we're later sorry about. And much of the blame lies with the way we live.

THE PRICE OF SCANDAL HAS GONE DOWN

The loss of community, the perception that "everyone does it," the fall from grace of so many of our leaders and role models that we looked up to, the desire for instant gratification, and the rise of a disposable society have all resulted in a lowering of the price of scandal.

Former New York governor Eliot Spitzer has been making more and more public appearances of late and has written numerous Op-Ed pieces as well. In what might be charitably described as hubris, he's actually lectured at Harvard on—you guessed it—ethics. In fact, Spitzer now co-hosts a talk show on CNN with Kathy Parker. By definition, he's forgiven. The lesson is clear. If you apologize profusely and lay low for a while you will be forgiven and even rewarded.

Who would have thought that possible two years ago? In fact, it seems as if the bigger the name, the faster we forgive and with good reason. First, the famous are worth more on the open market. Second, if our heroes do these things and get away with them, then that means it's okay for us lesser mortals.

This is certainly not the way it used to be. In the past, you at least had to do some prison time or study in a seminary for a while before you could be considered "rehabilitated." When Nixon was forced to resign, he did not get his own TV show. And unlike Bill Clinton after his affair with Monica Lewinsky, he did not resume his travels as a world-class statesman.

The fact is ours has become a society where the price of scandal is much lower than it used to be. We have, it seems, gradually devalued all the things that scandal destroys: one's good standing in the community, with family, in the workplace, at church. They're just not worth that much. Besides, with increased mobility comes the possibility of reinventing yourself elsewhere, especially if you're not famous, but simply a little guy who with no public persona. And let's not forget the snowball effect. The more people think it's okay to act this way, the more okay it becomes, and the more often it happens. There are no fewer than three governors since Spitzer's fall who have acted stupidly—David Paterson, Rod Blagojevich, and Mark Sanford. And then you have John Edwards, Charles Rangel, Hugh Grant, David Letterman, Sean Penn, Kobe Bryant, Halle Berry, and so many others.

Even a convicted and notorious murderer like David "Son of Sam" Berkowitz, who killed six people and wounded seven others in New York City, can find some measure of redemption. A July 13, 2010 article in the *New York Times* reported on a whole slew of respectable people who have become his friends. Titled "Admirers Make Over the Image of a Killer," the article describes how perfectly respectable individuals, including an attorney, a minister, and a TV host have befriended and helped Berkowitz. The common denominator is that most are Evangelical Christians. This is not surprising since "getting religion" and thereby being saved has long been one of the chief vehicles for achieving respectability and forgiveness for one's transgressions.

In the coming chapters we'll talk about individual factors, like arrogance, greed, honor, looking for the easy way out, insecurity, obsessive behavior, and so on. These are real reasons that explain dumb and irrational behavior. But a society that accepts such behavior in general, creates an environment where people are far more apt to use these as reasons even when their validity is questionable. And so in this way, social and individual traits reinforce each other and make such acts easier to commit.

2

ARROGANCE

"**A** One-Way Ticket to Disaster," the *New York Times* headline gleefully proclaimed. What were they talking about? you might wonder. The evils of underage drinking? Investing in the mortgage market? The seemingly endless war in Iraq? None of the above, it turns out.

The focus of this end-of-2007 piece was the seemingly incredible, yet entirely believable, tendency of our heroes, icons, and even role models to self-destruct, to do the kinds of things that we know *we* would never do were we in their shoes. And all in one year.

A United States senator, Larry Craig of Utah, solicits sex by signaling the occupant of a neighboring stall in a public restroom. Don Imus, a megastar in the talk-show world, calls members of the Rutgers University women's basketball team a bunch of "nappy-headed hos." Michael Vick, star quarterback for the Atlanta Falcons, risks his $130 million contract when he is convicted of dog fighting. Former supermodel Anna Nicole Smith dies from an overdose of sleeping pills and prescription drugs. Britney Spears, Lindsay Lohan, Paris Hilton, and so many others, engage in seemingly inexplicable behavior.

Had the headline appeared three months later, it would have been a perfect title for the disgrace and downfall of New York state governor Eliot Spitzer. At first, he might look like an unlikely member of this club. Spitzer and Spears rarely make the same celebrity gossip pages. And their humiliating falls from grace make for paper-thin similarities, easy to distinguish in the details. Read the news in 2009, and we have the sordid drama of Bernard Madoff, the dysfunction of New York State's government, the very public affair of Governor Mark Sanford. Each year is different, yet in a fundamental way, similar. Boneheaded behavior will always be with us.

There is, as it turns out, something much deeper that these examples share, not only with each other, but with a certain breed of successful personalities everywhere. By the time they exploded into the public eye, they had already taken many steps down a path that began harmlessly enough, months, or even years, earlier. But theirs was a path that should have been marked with a signpost echoing the *Times* headline: a one-way ticket to disaster. In fact, it's a path that people take innocently all the time, unaware of any lurking danger.

Arrogance is obviously not limited to the glamorous. On April 23, 1985, after years of planning and countless focus groups, Coca-Cola unveiled its new product to the world. "New Coke," as we now know, was a colossal bust. The calls complaining about it poured into company headquarters at the rate of about 7,000 a week.

After months of being skewered in the press and made fun of on late night TV shows, Coke gave in to reality and returned the original Coke to its rightful owners, the public. It was renamed Coca Cola Classic, but the only really classic thing about it was their mistake. The marketing mavens had heard but not listened to their research results. Consumers told them they loved Coke, not just for its taste, but because they felt a deep attachment to the brand name itself. Call it "Monday-morning quarterbacking," but, regardless, it was one of the worst marketing decisions ever, reflecting a certain degree of arrogance, coupled with amazingly poor judgment.

ARROGANCE IS EVERYWHERE

There must be a million cases of bad judgment a day in America. People insult other people and lose customers, friends, and jobs. They make bad purchases, investments, and agreements. They misinterpret what people are thinking and saying and others do the same to them. Why?

So I've been in Korea for about a week and a half now and what can I say. LIFE IS GOOD. I've got a spanking brand-new 3 bedroom apartment. Why do I need 3 bedrooms? Good question . . . The main bedroom is for my queen size bed . . . where CHUNG is going to [expletive] every hot chick in Korea over the next two years (5 down, 1,000,000,000 left to go) . . . the second bedroom is for my harem of chickies, and the third bedroom is for all of you [expletive] when you come out to visit my ass in Korea. I pretty much get about, on average, 5- to 8 phone numbers a night and at least 3 hot chicks that say they want to go home with me every night I go out. . . . I have bankers calling me every day with opportunities and they pretty much cater to my every whim—you know, golfing events, lavish dinners, a night out clubbing. Oh, by the way, someone's gotta start FedExing me boxes of [condoms]. I brought out about forty, but I think I'll run out of them by Saturday. Laters, Chung.

Move over Bill Clinton, Tiger Woods, Wilt Chamberlain, and all you other reputed men-about-town! You've met your match, if not in the number of women you reportedly conquered, then in sheer arrogance. Peter Chung may not have been a household name but he was well known in the financial world.

Chung moved up fast at Merrill-Lynch. He had impeccable credentials, having graduated from Princeton. The stodgy Carlyle Group sent him to Seoul, Korea, in 2001 to work in investments. The above is an e-mail this twenty-four-year-old *macho* man sent to his friends, shortly after he arrived in that bustling metropolis.

His bragging wouldn't have attracted much attention had it been limited to private conversation. But, as everyone knows, once you e-mail something, you never know where it will end up. His supposed buddies were so impressed, or more likely, unimpressed, by his sheer nerve that they e-mailed it to, well, the entire immediate world. And why not? He hadn't exactly made it sound like it was a secret. The forward box carried the title "Amazing Cautionary Tale." Sure enough, the Carlyle Group found out about Chung's assessment of Korean nightlife and his "resignation" followed very shortly thereafter.

When somebody does something really stupid, those around him or her feel totally justified in talking about it. It's almost as if they derive pleasure from gossiping but also need verification from others that it's indeed as dumb as they think it is. If you've done something foolish, only close friends or family will protect you and even they may abandon you if they think what you've done is too far out or evidence that you're out of touch.

Yet arrogant things are done all the time, by the high and mighty and by the not so high and mighty. It can describe your former classmate or cousin; your neighbor or fellow coworker. It goes by various names and has a long history. The ancient Greeks called it *hubris*, the Jews have dubbed it *chutzpah*, and the most common word for it is arrogance. It is the cause of many acts of folly and has brought down innumerable people. Yet it continues to exist right on up to the present day. Even as you're reading this book, any number of people are falling victim to its excesses. And since it affects so many of us, it's important to understand its causes.

Donald Trump, Madonna, Arnold Schwarzenegger, and many other larger-than-life personalities have used arrogance as a kind of currency. Trial lawyers, especially in personal injury law, actually advertise this quality. They seem defiant and blustering, but they also display, if you look closely enough, a keen awareness of the effects of their arrogance. It propels them. It persuades us that they are powerful enough to break the ordinary rules. They want to be seen as audacious, and they succeed.

What singled out people like Chung, and his more famous counterparts, like former president Clinton and ex-governor Spitzer, was the destructive nature of their arrogance—and their obliviousness to its inevitable outcome. They not only blithely ignored public standards, but they did so in violation of the savvy they already possessed. They had, after all, risen to success in organizations and systems whose rules they now flouted.

WHY ARROGANCE LEADS TO DUMB BEHAVIOR

It's a complicated question because the reasons are multiple and even overlapping, at times acting in concert with each other. Basically, they include the following nine factors:

1. Believing you're untouchable
2. Overconfidence
3. Obliviousness to others
4. Narcissism
5. A need to dominate
6. A crusader mentality
7. Rage
8. Rigidity
9. Society

Now, let's look at each one in turn, keeping in mind that an individual can exhibit more than one of these characteristics.

BELIEVING YOU'RE UNTOUCHABLE

Clinton didn't just have sex with someone other than his wife; he did it in the White House, about as public a place as you can find, a sure sign that he thought he was untouchable. Spitzer didn't just patronize a high-priced hooker. He did so exactly in the way that others had done when, as Attorney General, he caught and prosecuted them. But Clinton and Spitzer are very different in terms of their personalities, needs, and motives. We begin with a closer historical look at the former president.

It was 1980 and Fidel Castro had deported one hundred and twenty thousand Cubans, many of them criminals and political prisoners. They set sail for the United States seeking asylum and when they arrived, President Jimmy Carter had a real problem figuring out where to send them. Among those he turned to was his friend, Bill Clinton, who was then-governor of Arkansas. Clinton reluctantly agreed to help and about twenty thousand refugees were promptly transported to Fort Chaffee. The locals were furious. "Who needs these foreigners, these criminals in our fine state?" they asked.

Clinton was locked in a tight reelection race for governor with Frank White, his Republican opponent and the Cuban affair quickly became an issue, especially when some of the new arrivals escaped from the fort and frightened local residents. In the end, White, who had been twenty points behind in the polls before the Cubans came to the state, won the election. Clinton became the first governor in twenty-five years to lose a reelection campaign in Arkansas. Needless to say, he was stunned and bitterly disappointed.

Shortly thereafter, I received a call from a market research company asking if I wanted to go to Arkansas and help Clinton figure out why he lost and what he could do to prevent it from happening again. I agreed and a few days later, headed down to Little Rock with two colleagues. We met with Bill's people in a barbecue joint in Little Rock, where we were given an assessment of the problem and then drove to the city of Jonesboro the next day to conduct focus groups.

What we found was that people had rejected Clinton at the polls primarily because of a license tag fee they thought was unfair and because of the Cuban debacle. We also discovered that voters objected to Hillary using the name of Rodham without adding Clinton to it. A farmer from eastern Arkansas with whom I spoke expressed it rather succinctly: "If Clinton can't get his wife to take his name, then he's not in control of his wife. And if he can't control his wife, how in the hell is he gonna be able to run the state?"

Clinton badly wanted to get elected again. And he knew that if he lost this time his career would probably be over. He also knew something else: the odds were against him. The pundits, the polls, the headlines all spelled disaster. But when we met with him, there was an unmistakable determination. Clinton genuinely believed victory was his—if he played it right, if he changed course. His confidence was infectious and it energized us. The question we were asked to answer by the Clinton people was whether or not he should admit that he'd made mistakes. Would he look weak if he did so? After traveling the length and width of the state talking with people, we presented our findings to the staff and made our recommendations.

It was our view that Arkansans were, by and large, plainspoken people who wanted to be told the truth. Therefore, Clinton should own up to the mistakes of the past and tell the people that he'd learned from them. Equally important, his wife should be known from now on as Hillary Rodham Clinton. Other people influential in Clinton's life, like Dick Morris and Vernon Jordan, agreed.

Bill Clinton followed our advice and readily agreed that he'd done some wrong things in the past, but had learned his lesson. "My daddy never had to whip me twice for the same thing," he said. He won and the rest is history. The point is Clinton displayed no arrogance here. He ate humble pie, as they say. This was in sharp contrast to his handling of the Monica Lewinsky affair in which he blustered "I did not have sex with that woman." How did it happen that a man who readily admitted his failings did the opposite some thirteen years later? Sure, he eventually acknowledged that what he did was "immoral and foolish." But even then he had to lash out at his critics for even demanding an answer from him. And his initial gut reaction was to deny any wrongdoing.

It's a complicated question, but there's no doubt that arrogance played a major role in his response. He was now President of the United

States, arguably the most powerful man in the world. In the old days, he was merely a defeated Arkansas governor. Looking at what subsequently happened, it seemed dumb for him to have thought he could get away with it. But then again, looking at his past, why not? Over the years, people like Clinton have needed to convince themselves that they're different from ordinary folks, that they can win against long odds. Often he did win, but sometimes he lost, as with the Monica Lewinsky case, and when he did it cost him heavily.

As he eventually admitted, Clinton had sex with Gennifer Flowers on numerous occasions and an Arkansas state trooper testified that he'd had sex with many other women while in office. More importantly, he'd never been punished for it. So even though he was now in his most visible office, the past did suggest that even when people are watching you, you can get away with it. He not only had sex with Monica in the White House, but also reportedly made advances toward another woman he knew, Kathleen Willey, when she was at the White House for a visit. Willey said she rebuffed his overtures; Clinton denied having made any.

But the times had changed and Clinton did not get away with it. He was impeached by the House of Representatives in December 1998 on allegations of obstruction of justice and perjury. Although a more forgiving Senate voted to acquit, he became the first president in over a century to have impeachment attached to his record. Years later, he left little doubt about his justification. In an interview for the CBS program *60 Minutes,* Clinton said with respect to Lewinsky: "I did something for the worst possible reason. Just because I could." It was to be a memorable quote. Then he added, "I think that's just about the most morally indefensible reason anybody could have for doing anything."

One of the major changes in the United States was the attitude toward hanky-panky committed by those in high office. Fifty years ago, the dalliances of Kennedy and Johnson were considered pretty off-limits. Reporters knew about them, but there was still a view that such matters were private, at least as far as the mainstream media was concerned. But during the Clinton years, that no longer seemed to hold true. Perhaps it was the increasingly fierce competition to make news, or maybe respect for the institution of the presidency had declined.

Technology played a role too. There was DNA—remember the stain on Monica's blue dress? Also, the quality of filming and taping had improved dramatically. The Internet meant that juicy stories could be spread far more quickly and broadly, aided by legions of bloggers looking for attention. There were no longer any physical boundaries to communication. This made it very difficult to squelch, let alone manage, anything and certainly not salacious stories about the President of the United States. As a result, the chances of being conclusively caught were far better than they'd been in decades past. Clinton couldn't run and he couldn't hide. Like a deer crossing a country road at night, he was caught in the headlights.

As psychologists will tell you, the signs foretelling such behavior can often be found in one's past, if we look for them. And in Bill Clinton's case, there was at least one early hint that this area might become a problem, well before his long string of Arkansas escapades. While at Yale, Clinton wrote to a close friend who'd asked him for help in getting a coveted White House Fellowship:

> About the White House Fellowships, the best story I know on them is that virtually the only non-conservative who ever got one was a quasi-radical woman who wound up in the White House sleeping with LBJ, who made her wear a peace symbol around her waist whenever they made love. You may go far, Cliff; I doubt you will ever go that far!

At the very least we see that the idea of a president sleeping with someone in the White House was by no means unthinkable and the kind of thing "a bad boy" like Clinton might well do. There is also a suggestion here of humiliation and conquest in the sense that this woman, who opposed LBJ's war policies, would nevertheless sleep with him. What it may have suggested to Clinton is that the President was king and could do whatever he wanted.

Clinton was far from the only politician to have displayed conceit in his pursuit of pleasure. The list is endless. At a certain point people do what they want to do and "let the public be damned," as they say. Take Mark Foley, a six-term Florida congressman. A Republican, he resigned in 2006 after being exposed for having sent sexually explicit messages via the Internet. But this was not your garden-variety pervert. Not only was he a powerful legislator, but his prey of choice was under-age Congressional pages. Now that took nerve. As the *New York Times* reporters who wrote the story observed, "And he might have known he would be watched."

There has to be a good deal of arrogance of power in a man who thinks he can blithely e-mail Congressional pages and not be found out, especially since pages had been victimized in the past. Given their youth, naïveté, and absence of any clout in a world that runs on clout, it's not surprising that they would be. The following exchange suggests a man who, it seems, couldn't care less what anyone thought:

Foley: "What ya wearing?"

Page: "Tshirt and shorts."

Foley: "Love to slip them off you."

In looking at Foley's history, we can see that it isn't only the position of power that makes such people feel invincible. The *speed* with which they become successful can also be a factor. Foley's rise in politics was very rapid. And when that happens, people can feel even more omnipotent. They believe that they are mysteriously, yet undoubtedly, destined for great success. This makes them lose touch with reality. Oh yes, Foley said the right things when apprehended: "I am deeply sorry and I apologize for letting down my family and the people of Florida I have had the privilege to represent." But you have to wonder, was he sorry for what he did or that he was caught?

At twenty-eight, Ryan Karben was the youngest assemblyman in New York State history. Talk about a meteoric rise. He had already served two terms in the Rockland County legislature and became a member of the Ramapo Township planning board at the ripe old age of eighteen. It looked like he could go very far, very fast in politics. And then, quicker than you could say Mark Foley or Gary Hart, it all dissolved in a heap of sexual allegations that left the prim and proper Orthodox Jewish community he came from and represented, in a state of shock.

What he had done wasn't all that terrible, compared to the misdeeds of some other politicians. He was accused of having brought three Assembly interns to his home, where they watched pornography together. It wasn't the pornography that upset people as much as the fact that interns are vulnerable and relatively powerless. Aware of and sensitive to this, the Assembly had a policy forbidding any socializing by its members with interns.

Karben graduated from the prestigious Columbia University Law School and people were shocked at his lack of judgment. They thought a smart guy like him should know better, but being smart and being restrained don't always go together. A former partner at Karben's law firm commented sadly, "I was surprised when I heard that he resigned from the Assembly and I was even more surprised when I heard the allegations against him. It seemed very out of character."

Karben was described as "a shining star" by Nicole Doliner, secretary of the Clarkstown Democratic Committee in Rockland County. "He was very inspiring. He would give a speech and you would say, 'Wow, let's go.' He really believed in what he said." And he had told others that he believed he could be governor of New York State one day. Maybe he could have, but we'll never find out.

The Foley and Karben cases both broke in 2006, a coincidence, but the similarities between them are striking. Both individuals rise very quickly in politics and both are toppled by sexual allegations. Those whom they are charged with abusing are young and powerless. More-over, the communities they represent—Monsey and Spring Valley in Karben's case and Palm Beach in Foley's—are on the conservative side.

They should have realized the possible consequences of their ac-tions, given their constituencies and the fact that elected officials al-ways have people waiting in the wings who can benefit from their downfall. Think of the shame and embarrassment they must have felt. Think of the potential they had for going further. When we consider that, we see how much they truly lost. Both fell victim to a fatal com-bination of arrogance and a feeling of being untouchable. Its likely source? The very power they had.

There are times, though, when you have enough power to with-stand the moral onslaught and survive, however diminished your reputation may be. Consider the case of Utah's senator Larry Craig, another politician with a conservative constituency. Rumors had cir-culated for years about Craig's sexual orientation. Yet that didn't stop him from soliciting gay sex in a public restroom. And in a Minneapolis airport, no less. Talk about lack of discretion!

It's true, American society is a lot more liberal now than it was forty years ago. I recall going to a gay bar called The Grapevine, in East St. Louis, Illinois, back in 1968 with a fellow graduate student, Laud Humphreys. Gay himself, Humphreys wanted to show me what the gay scene was like. East St. Louis was a down-at-the-heels city then and the area we went to was industrial and pretty desolate. It was a time when gays were at the outer margins of respectability. His disser-tation, which later became the path-breaking and controversial book, *The Tearoom Trade*, consisted of interviewing gays who were often passing as straights.

The problem is that for Senator Craig, who represents "Mormon Country," such behavior may still be viewed the way it was in Hum-phreys' time. Had Craig been Barney Frank from liberal Massachusetts, it would have been a totally different story. So, to preserve his standing in conservative Utah, Craig fought back, asserting that the police had entrapped him.

If we're to understand why those in power abuse it, it's important to realize how much gratification and validation they derive from being on top. Say you're a judge. Imagine how it feels when everyone rises as you walk in, and must sit silent and attentive, as long as you're in that courtroom. Your flowing black robes add to the feeling of omnipotence. They mark you as a person of distinction.

Even more significant is what you do. You determine who shall remain free and who shall not. People fawn all over you. Lawyers try to figure out how to get on your good side, how to influence you. And when you sentence someone, those present hang on your every word, especially if it's a celebrated case. Is it any surprise that you feel all-powerful? And is it shocking if such feelings can lead to excesses that can return to haunt you if you've gone too far?

The same is true when you make a lot of money. Years ago, in 1991, the famed Stew Leonard, whose dairy corporation bore his name, was charged with $17 million in massive financial fraud. The disc that powered the fraud was hidden inside a hollowed-out book, the oodles of cash in an innocuous looking fireplace. Some of the money, which ended up in the Caribbean, was put inside what looked like innocent baby gifts. The point is Leonard's company was highly visible. But great success is often an aphrodisiac that makes those who have it miscalculate how easily they can fall from grace. What can you expect from a place named "The World's Largest Dairy Store," by Ripley's Believe It or Not! For those curious about the outcome, Leonard received a four-year sentence for the scheme.

Clinton, Craig, and Leonard are among the most flagrant and well-known cases of arrogance, but it's all around us. A couple marries. One comes from money, the other doesn't. The rich one lords it over the other, maintaining control over the purse strings, perhaps by insisting on separate accounts. After years of this, the tables suddenly turn when he or she falls ill and is forced to depend on the one with no money. The long-suffering spouse is now the dominant one and feels it's time for payback.

You head a branch of a large company located hundreds of miles from corporate headquarters. You get used to the near-absolute power you wield. Because of your autocratic nature, no one criticizes you for fear of losing his or her job. One day, the overall head of the company pays a visit to see how things are going. She criticizes you, and, forgetting your place, you vehemently defend yourself to the point where you anger her. The next thing you know she calls you "an arrogant know-it-all," and gives you the boot.

OVERCONFIDENCE AND TEMPTING FATE

When people act arrogantly, what they usually seem to imply by their actions is that they don't give a damn what anybody else thinks and, what's more, they don't have to. As we have seen, they often miscalculate. But what causes them to miscalculate? Research has been done on this question and it shows that people generally overestimate their ability to control things. People will, for example, often take a hard line in negotiations with employees. Then, when the employees go on strike they express genuine surprise. A person will say to someone: "If you don't stop harassing me, I'll take you to court." The other person, overconfident that this won't happen, continues in his behavior and is then surprised to find himself the object of a lawsuit, or worse.

What is happening here, in addition to a failure to see the other side, is a refusal to view one's own situation from the perspective of anyone else involved. There is a resistance to "reality checks" from outside. Not surprisingly, when players in a chess game are told, in the middle of the game, to switch sides, they come up with strategies and moves they had no idea existed when they were playing their own position.

When it comes to tempting fate, political consultants don't usually make dumb comments. They're paid to stop their clients from making them. Ed Rollins has served as an adviser to Ronald Reagan, Ross Perot, and numerous political aspirants for office. One of them was Republican Christine Todd Whitman, who narrowly beat Jim Florio in the 1993 New Jersey gubernatorial race.

After the election, Rollins spoke with journalists and made some pretty asinine comments. In effect, he told them that the campaign spent half a million dollars to get black ministers to *not* promote Florio's candidacy and to ensure that Democratic campaign workers would stay home on election day. As he put it: "We basically said to ministers who had endorsed Florio, 'Do you have a special project?'" Contributions were then made to "their favorite charities." Going public with this information was not a smart move. Rollins' reputation suffered. What it reflects is that, like Clinton, Karben and so many others, Rollins let his success blind him to the standards of others. As a result, he saw no reason to fight the urge to crow a bit once he felt relaxed after a strenuous effort. In other words, he was overconfident. Rollins signed on in December 2007 to help run Mike Huckabee's campaign. And we know how poorly Huckabee did.

Another very well-known case was former Colorado senator Gary Hart, who ran for the Democratic presidential nomination in 1988. A Yale Law School graduate, he was no dummy. And yet, after stories surfaced that he was having an affair, Hart did something ridiculous, considering that he knew he was guilty before anyone else did. He told the media: "Follow me around. I don't care. . . . Put a tail on me. They'll be very bored."

Well, the media did exactly that and struck pay-dirt almost immediately, publishing a photo of a young woman leaving Hart's home at night in Washington D.C. Several days later, they were given photos by someone of twenty-nine-year-old model Donna Rice playfully balanced on Gary Hart's knees aboard a yacht. The story told of them having spent a night in Bimini aboard the yacht. It didn't help that the yacht's name was *Monkey Business*. Hart became a national laughing-stock and dropped out of the race in which he had, until becoming undone, been the odds-on-favorite. He must have done some serious soul searching, receiving a doctorate in politics from Oxford in 2001. Proof that being smart and having smarts aren't the same thing.

What's noteworthy about the Hart case isn't his lustful trysts. It's that he dared the press to expose him. Such overconfident bluster would ill-become even a priest with a squeaky-clean record. And Hart was no priest. Yet his own experience—rather than teach him a worldly appreciation of the risks of public office—reinforced a sense of near-invincibility. The fruits of exceptionally sharp judgment early in life came back to poison that judgment later on. Hart had become arrogant.

A more recent case of overreaching was that of General Stanley McChrystal. In a now famous interview given to *Rolling Stone* magazine, the general muses over how he could dismiss Joseph Biden with a good one-liner: "Are you asking about Vice President Biden?" McChrystal says, laughing. "Who's that?"

"Biden?" is the mocking response by a top adviser: "Did you say: Bite Me?" McChrystal is also dismissive of senior adviser Richard Holbrooke. "Oh, not another e-mail from Holbrooke. I don't even want to open it," he says.

In the *Rolling Stone* article, McChrystal's staff is described as "a handpicked collection of killers, spies, geniuses, patriots, political operators, and outright maniacs" who "pride themselves on their can-do attitude and their disdain for authority." Sources close to him say that the general thought President Obama looked "intimidated" at a meeting with top military leaders and that he "didn't seem very engaged," when McChrystal first met with him, one on one.

This interview was the precipitating factor in Obama's decision to dump McChrystal. But why did McChrystal throw caution to the winds? The answer lies in McChrystal's basic personality. Obama didn't know much about the man he appointed. If he had, he would have learned that McChrystal piled up more than nineteen hundred hours of demerits for insubordination, partying, and drinking as a student at West Point.

Throughout his career, McChrystal had operated on the belief that confrontation wins the day. Tellingly, he had pressured the President into committing far more troops than he had originally intended. Who wouldn't feel supremely confident after that? There was also the fact that McChrystal often operated in areas where there was no one to second-guess him. He had, for example, run the Pentagon's most secretive "black-ops" for five years.

McChrystal expressed deep regret about the interview, most probably not out of remorse, but because it cost him his job. He had miscalculated, a victim of the arrogance of power that leads to overconfidence.

OBLIVIOUS TO OTHERS

"He came from nothing and now look at him!" people will declaim. In a way, the distance traveled can also impact on the degree of arrogance. This is because when you arrive, there is an almost exaggerated perception of how far you've actually come. For Bill Clinton, the road to fame and power began when he was a poor child in a backwater town with the wistful name of Hope. When he got to the White House it was literally Wonderland, and Wonderland can lead to the delusion that you are impervious to criticism or harm.

In a celebrated case, Mel Gibson put his foot in his mouth with respect to offending Jews. Arrested for drunk driving, he cursed out the officer, who was Jewish, and Jews in general. "Jews are responsible for all wars in the world," he ranted. Sure, people say lots of things when they're drunk, but there's usually more to it. We often read of sober prominent people who are arrested and verbally abuse the officers. "Do you know who I am?" is one typical response.

This happens because the rich and powerful live in their own world, one where their wealth and power make them oblivious to much of what's going on. They are used to getting away with berating underlings and making outrageous remarks. Some researchers believe that those who have power focus so intensely on the perks of power—fame, money, easily available sex—that they don't even notice most of the people around them or how they might be perceived by them. These lesser individuals, often gofers, say nothing, of course, because they have no power and just want to keep their jobs.

Wouldn't we call the celebrity publicist Lizzie Grubman clueless and arrogant? Asked to move her Mercedes out of a fire lane in front of a Hamptons nightclub, Grubman became enraged and drove the vehicle into a crowd of people, injuring sixteen of them. As she stepped on the gas, people claimed to have heard her yelling "white trash" at the club bouncer who'd asked her to move on. She then drove away into the night. Grubman pleaded guilty to assault charges and apologized to her victims, but the media expressed skepticism as to her sincerity.

You don't even have to be terribly influential to commit these types of miscues. It's enough to just think you are. How about the arrogant Richard Judd, former president of Central Connecticut State University in New Britain, Connecticut? He was forced to retire after it was revealed that he had copied from various sources, including the *New York Times*, in a column he penned for the *Hartford Courant*. And that wasn't his only blunder. He'd also been busted for impersonating a cop when he stopped someone he thought was speeding. In his little universe, he was the absolute boss. What he forgot was that when he left that world, he was just another guy with a good job.

Even the powerless can display great arrogance. On January 23, 2008, a young woman named Micki appeared on the *Dr. Phil Show*. She was a habitual and convicted con artist. She told Dr. Phil that she had rejected a job offer at McDonald's because "I'm too smart to be flippin' burgers." The audience laughed and Dr. Phil retorted, "Lady, you're living in your car, *living in your car*. You've farmed out your kids to friends. You have such a feeling of entitlement." Upon hearing and absorbing this Micki burst into tears and admitted that she had the wrong attitude.

NARCISSUS LIVES

Narcissus is famous in Greek mythology for having fallen in love with his own reflection in a pool. And therefore, when someone is deemed by others to be totally self-centered they're called *narcissistic*. While most powerful people are not pure narcissists, a good number manifest such tendencies. Blinded by an inflated sense of self-importance and an accompanying inability to accept criticism, they are thus prone to foolish decisions.

Among the politicians most-often accused of this kind of self-absorption was Richard Nixon. When rejected, his narcissism turned inward. After losing the 1960 election to John F. Kennedy, he famously and bitterly remarked: "Now you won't have Nixon to kick around any more." In one of his most memorable roles on *Saturday Night Live,* comedian-turned-senator Al Franken played the part of a man who thinks the entire world revolves around him. In his typical monologue, Franken would say things like: "What have you done for *me,* Al Franken?" Now he can ask former senator Norm Coleman, who he beat in Minnesota, that question.

Dr. Nechama Liss-Levenson, a noted psychologist practicing in Long Island characterized the syndrome in the following terms:

> There are those who do wrong things because they feel there's a separate set of rules for them. They're often people who had authoritarian parents. Stereotypically, the father comes home and gets whatever he wants. Rules are made according to his whims. So the child can be led to think, 'When I grow up it's going to be done *my* way.' It's an internalization of the idea that there are special rules for 'special people.'

And such people can overreach and mess up. That would certainly be the case for twenty-three-year-old Wesley Ridgwell, who went through an incredible 705 Florida tollbooths without bothering to pay. His reaction to the charges? "I'm such a good person. People who know me just can't believe this is happening." Obviously, the arresting officers who now know Wesley wouldn't agree with his narcissistic self-assessment.

Some people have what I would call an "arrogance of intelligence." One way in which this is acted out, with harmful consequences, is when such individuals believe that if you're really smart, you shouldn't have to work too much and that doing so means you're dumb. This can lead to all sorts of mistakes, like not reviewing material when you're supposed to, not preparing for meetings, and making enemies by ridiculing others who do work hard. These geniuses frequently end up having to take risks to cover up the poor performance that results from such attitudes. While many of these types are, in fact, smart, they fall into the category of what we popularly describe as "too smart for their own good."

Related to this is a sense, not only of higher intelligence, but of moral superiority. We have all met such types and we often accuse them of having "tunnel vision." They're people who believe they're right even when it's clear to most of us that they're wrong. Sometimes they end up on important committees or even juries and drive everyone nuts. Such people often rely on their intelligence to guide them. They are smart, they think; they've thought it through, as only they can. Therefore, they must be right.

A NEED TO DOMINATE

Both Clinton and Spitzer were superstars, with the latter being touted as potential presidential timbre as soon as he took office following his landslide victory. Both were brilliant and successful, boasting ivory tower credentials, yet remaining fully comfortable in the trenches of politics. They were each swept into office on a mandate of change. And both were brought down by tawdry sexual scandals.

But in truth, they couldn't have been more different. The fact that Spitzer used a prostitute is just the beginning, though that difference already speaks volumes about the larger ones, as we'll see. Unlike Clinton, Spitzer was never a charmer, a salesman, a seducer. He didn't win power; he seized it. While both were driven by destructive arrogance, their addictions were nearly opposite: Clinton desperately needed to seduce; Spitzer had to dominate.

In his studies of destructive leadership, the psychiatrist Vamik Volkan found that such leaders rose to power in a way that demonstrated an incredible ability to control their surroundings. Some manipulated by fear, others by charisma, still others by tactical ingenuity. But they all did so in what psychiatrists call "a hypomanic drive." They moved constantly, furiously, obsessively, and were never satisfied. They couldn't simply sit back and let things take their course, even when doing so was to their advantage. They had a way of seizing opportunities, rather than waiting for them. This pattern is a perfect description of Eliot Spitzer and its roots can be found in his childhood.

When Spitzer was a boy in the exclusive Fieldston enclave of Riverdale, New York, his parents held him to a bizarre nightly ritual at the dinner table. He and his siblings had to come with a well-researched point to argue. Every night. The experience was as formative an education as anything he encountered at Princeton and Harvard years later. Spitzer grew to be an exacting logician, a furious debater more at home in the pure science of argument than the muddy waters of human influence. He learned to control his environment by outsmarting his opponents, by emerging as "the cleverest guy in the room," as one critic would later put it. If he didn't win the love of his peers, he won their admiration and agreement, or, perhaps, their submission.

BEWARE THE CRUSADER

In his rise to power, the use of moral principles to make people toe the line became Spitzer's trademark. As attorney general, he became a crusader. There's nothing wrong with that. Martin Luther King was a crusader and so was Ralph Nader. The problem here is when you are an overzealous crusader and that's what Spitzer was. He lashed out at corrupt tycoons and more common criminals with all the single-mindedness and certainty of a small-town preacher. He used statutory regulations, threats and pressure to bend people to his will. And it worked. He took an especially hard line against "Johns" who picked up prostitutes. He pushed to get their sentences legally extended, from three months to ten months. Nobody picked up on the signs.

Spitzer's temptations were not yet known, but he was clearly not one to brook any disagreement. As he told a minority assemblyman, "I'm a fucking steamroller, and I'll roll over you." Soon after taking office, he suffered his first scandal. Called "Troopergate," it involved charges, largely proven, that Spitzer's staff used state police to investigate his main Republican rival, state Senator Joseph Bruno. Although Spitzer survived the scandal, his armor was permanently chinked. He had lost the luster of a crusader, a pure reformer. Now he was a flawed figure, and the press gave him no slack. He could no longer force the public to view him in his own image. His public persona was out of control. For most politicians, that's just reality.

Shortly after Troopergate broke, Spitzer sought to go after another Republican rival. Now, however, the issue was debated among his staff, with one adviser asking if maybe they should cool it. Should they hold back a few months, or at least weeks? "Nah," Spitzer replied, according to the *New Yorker*. "If it's right, it's right."

The article in which that quote appears is oddly titled, "The Humbling of Eliot Spitzer," and it appeared in the *New Yorker* six months before the scandal that shamed him out of office. I say oddly because in the piece Spitzer appears anything but humbled. During an in-flight interview with the reporter, Nick Paumgarten, Spitzer complained about his recent treatment in the press. But he took a moment to confess that on these private flights, when he looks down at New York State from above the clouds, he has the following thought: "Mine, all mine." Asked what was the best advice he ever received, Spitzer answered, "Ignore most of the advice we're giving you."

This is precisely the language of someone who has already begun to rebel against the uncontrollable murkiness of the outside world, and retreat into one of his own making. It's the thinking of someone who resents having to suddenly live by the standards of others, after being served so well by imposing his own. Something of his former influence had begun to slip. So he became the ultimate flouter of standards—not just legal but practical standards as well. He took "Kristen" and, with her consent, apparently played rough. He took her as if to say, to himself more than anyone, "I really am beyond their control—because look what I can do."

With each act of defiance—of the very standards he himself created and imposed—he reaffirmed what the world had begun to deny him. Spitzer could do as he pleased; he was an enforcer of principle, of the code, and what better way to show it than to act above it? It is not clear whether his illicit behavior grew more fierce and bold with his public "humbling." He reportedly had been seeing prostitutes for years. But far more striking about his recent behavior was its destructively arrogant nature: he acted as though he was far too powerful to trifle over finding a credible alias or a more discrete payment method.

RAGE

"I just lost it," is what people often say when describing how they got angry. It's really a way of claiming temporary insanity when you think about it. What it means is if you hadn't lost it, then you'd be the real you—calm, rational, and responsible. When people are angry they tend to act impulsively, often with embarrassing results.

That's what happened when actor Russell Crowe struck a SoHo, New York, hotel clerk with a telephone when he couldn't get a call placed fast enough to his wife in Australia. Blaming his arrogant outburst on jet lag and loneliness, Crowe called the confrontation one of the "most shameful" of his life, adding "and I've done some pretty dumb things in my life."

Gary Anthony Ramsay was a reporter and weekend anchor for *NY1 News*, a pretty good job. Watching a different show on his channel about Bernard Kerik, hosted by colleague John Schiumo, he became incensed by callers asserting that Hillary Clinton had played a prominent role in the investigation of Kerik, one that had embarrassed her rival, Rudolph Giuliani. Ramsay called in to complain vociferously. Fine. You can do that. Oprah Winfrey called in to *Larry King Live* with a complaint about his treatment of his guest, James Frey. But she used her real name and Ramsay, as it happened, didn't.

Instead, he gave a name as phony as a three dollar bill—"Dalton, from the Upper East Side." *Dalton*, as in the Dalton School on 89th Street and Park Avenue? Was that a joke, or just the first name that came to mind? Whatever the reason, he received a call after the show from the host, John Schiumo, who told Ramsay he'd recognized him. Why not? He worked with the guy and Ramsay had not really tried to change his voice. Ramsay apologized for what he called his "lapse in judgment." The next day he resigned, a fifteen-year career seriously harmed all because he got mad and "lost it." The station claimed "he was ready for a move," but no one believed it.

RIGIDITY

Another cause of arrogance is rigidity. "Don't confuse me with facts, because I've already made up my mind," is an oft-heard refrain. I once worked on a marketing project where the concept was to introduce to the public a square potato chip, sort of a combination between a square-shaped cracker and a round potato chip. We did focus groups and they clearly showed that people didn't like this idea. As it happened though, the marketing manager who'd introduced it refused to give it up and insisted that it be produced and placed in the supermarket. It flopped, big time, and the one whose idea it was got the ax.

Other examples abound. A team loses game after game. The players show no enthusiasm on the court. Word gets around that the coach has lost the confidence of his players, that they aren't motivated. But the owner refuses to make a change. For him it would be a tacit admission that he had erred in hiring him. You refuse to sell a car you love that's a lemon even when you can. You keep an incompetent employee long after you should have let him go even though he keeps making costly mistakes. In common parlance, this is called "throwing good money after bad" and it happens all the time. They are more likely cases of stubbornness than arrogance, but they're in the same family of responses.

One of the most egregious instances of rigidity concerned a Manhattan Starbucks outlet. On 9/11, several ambulance workers went there to get some water for shock victims. To their amazement, store employees charged them $130 for the three cases they took. After being defensive initially, top management at Starbucks issued an apology and a refund, but one has to be amazed at the inflexibility of the employee who rang up the bill in the first place.

President Obama is an example of someone who cultivates an image of "coolness," of flexibility. Oh sure, he can become angry, but even there you sense that it may be done or presented as such for strategic effect. Take, for example, the announcement of new housing construction in Jerusalem while Vice President Joseph Biden was in Israel. The diplomatic gaffe turned into a full-blown crisis between the United States and its ally, with Obama reportedly "infuriated" to the point where he publicly humiliated Benjamin Netanyahu by refusing to welcome him to the White House while the Israeli leader was visiting the United States. Ultimately, however, at the urging of some of his closest advisers, Obama concluded that his declared goal of bringing about peace between Israel and the Palestinians would not be advanced by taking this tack. And so a month or so later, Netanyahu was reinvited to the White House and this time the visit was a love-fest, with plenty of photo-ops and feel-good comments by both leaders.

The approach is similar to that toward Iran. First, Obama tried to reach out to their government. But when the elections there turned into a farce and Iran clamped down harshly, with thousands of arrests and severe repression generally, Obama drew back and began talking about sanctions. He gave Iran until September 2009 to change its ways. When that deadline passed without much happening, the President gave them until January. The point is that he did not take drastic action.

In both cases, Obama has been a pragmatist. Whether or not this is the correct approach in the long run cannot be predicted, but, regardless, we see here that people can make threats and issue ultimatums and then change course. It is a strategy that reduces conflict and avoids irreversible errors. If more people adopted it, then the dumb things described in this book would happen with far less frequency.

George W. Bush's approach to such matters was entirely different. He waged an unpopular war in Iraq for years. He knew it would doom him politically, but he believed in what he was doing. The same was true of his invasion of Afghanistan. He was a staunch supporter of Israel despite fierce Arab opposition, especially his Saudi Arabian friends. It's not a question of whether or not he was right. History will judge both men. It's the attitude.

Culture can also play a role in rigidity. Toyota had received more than 2,000 complaints of unintended acceleration since 2002. Yet it was only in February 2010, after a particularly terrible accident, in which four people were killed when their Lexus burst into flames, that the company took serious action. Millions of vehicles were recalled and the production and sales of eight models were halted.

Stonewalling was not a smart strategy because the damage to its image cost Toyota dearly. So why did they refuse to act for so long? After all, Toyota's top executive, Yoshimi Inaba, had said, "Every day is a lesson and there is something to be learned. This was a hard lesson." Part of the answer may lie in Japan's corporate culture, which stems from Japanese culture itself.

In Japanese society, authority is highly respected and company loyalty is treasured. It is not the American ideal of rugged individualism that prevails, but rather the idea that one must conform and subordinate one's own wishes to the group. In such an environment, it becomes difficult for people in the know to speak out.

Unwillingness to consult with others is another symptom of a rigid personality. I learned a long time ago that if everybody tells you you're wrong then you probably are. But there are people who believe strongly in their "gut reactions," their intuition. This can work very well in many situations, as Malcolm Gladwell has shown in his book, *Blink,* but there are times when this approach needs to be abandoned.

Let's say you interview someone to be deputy director of your privately run senior citizens center and you like her a lot. Her responses impress you and you become excited about the prospect of her joining your management team. You feel like hiring her on the spot. All that remains is to check out her references. You do so and start hearing all sorts of negative things. She's disorganized, abrupt with people, not a team player. It's particularly upsetting because these are names the applicant gave you. So it can also be a sign that she has poor judgment. But you find one individual who thinks she's really great. And on that basis, you hire her. Alas, it turns out that all the bad things people said about her were on the money. Reluctantly, after three months, you are forced to terminate her. If only you'd listened to what others were saying.

THE ROLE OF SOCIETY

On a personal level, arrogance can at least be controlled. We'll have more to say about how in our concluding chapter. In the final analysis, though, the blame for the arrogance of individuals does not lie entirely with them. The society in which we live is equally culpable, for it has encouraged and rewarded them. Even now, we see that an impeached president is largely forgiven and respected. He speaks for six-figure sums, and with his wife serving as secretary of state, Bill is still very much a player, albeit a somewhat tarnished one. Two years after his downfall, Eliot Spitzer is a sought after television guest, where he discusses how he "just fell" into what he did wrong. Martha Stewart is a regular guest on major shows and Macy's carries her products.

When a minister sins Elmer Gantry-style and his congregation continues to support him; when a disgraced politician runs again for public office and wins; when sports heroes with tainted records are lionized; when people involved in financial scandals retain their standing in the community because they are still wealthy, it sends a clear message. That message, one attentively noted by the young and not-yet molded, is that if you commit serious wrongs you can still achieve redemption, especially if you're connected.

3

AMBITION AND GREED

One of the most notorious tales of ambition and obsession is that of the former New York State chief judge, Sol Wachtler. A charming, brilliant, and highly successful jurist, Wachtler had been touted as a likely gubernatorial candidate for the Republicans, even a possible vice presidential nominee.

It all came crashing down on him the day he was arrested and charged with harassing Joy Silverman, a socialite with whom he had a long-term affair. When she broke up with him, the judge could not accept it, so Wachtler initiated a campaign to win her back that included threatening phone calls and letters, all sent by an anonymous man who, it turned out, was his own creation. A frightened Silverman discussed the matter with him and he offered himself as the shining knight who would rescue her from this crazy person. In a celebrated case, the judge was tried, convicted, and sentenced to hard prison time.

Sol Wachtler was totally obsessed with Joy Silverman. In a biography about him, written with Wachtler's cooperation, a former colleague reflects, "He *had* to have adulation. He thrived on it. When he didn't get it, it was something he couldn't tolerate." And it was something that was within his reach, because he not only had talent and perseverance, but charisma. "With his attentive, ocean-blue eyes and seductive baritone," the author observes, "he had a way of making one feel like the most important person he had talked to all day, and then made a hundred others feel the same way."

Yet all that charm and intelligence failed to prevent even a judge from exercising bad judgment. Why? Because his emotions and desire to succeed at whatever he did were very powerful. He wanted Joy back so badly it literally clouded his thinking. This pattern developed early on in his life and was on display in his teenage years, too.

By his own admission, Wachtler was a terrible athlete. The small St. Petersburg, Florida, high school he attended started a basketball team. Despite his lack of talent, Sol was a popular kid and was elected team captain, though he really functioned as the manager. Shortly thereafter, his parents, anxious that he get into a good college, transferred him to a boarding school in Milford, Connecticut. On his transcript, under extracurricular activities, was the entry: "Captain, Varsity Basketball Team," words that would make any admissions director and, of course, coach, drool.

As soon as he arrived at Milford, young Wachtler was invited to come down to the gym and "shoot some hoops." The school, a power in the state league, had high hopes that he would be the final piece in their quest for a state championship. They were so excited that they gave him a uniform *before* seeing him play.

Wachtler took them up on it. Of course, he knew he was no good, so why did he do it? Because, as he put it, "For some strange reason I thought that I would not disappoint them. Although I knew I had no talent or ability, I believed that somehow, in some way, I would meet the challenge. Maybe I would get lucky—or maybe I would prove to be a natural. Or maybe, just maybe, through some magical or celestial intervention, I would astonish even myself with a performance worthy of their expectations."

It never happened. The coach tossed the ball to him and he dropped it. He was told to dribble the ball and discovered that he could not dribble and run at the same time. "Shoot!" the coach yelled. The ball left his hands and went under the backboard. Not even close. "Hook it!" shouted the coach. "There is no hook," responded Sol, having no idea what a hook shot was. Disappointed beyond belief, the coach said, "Turn in your uniform and lock up," and walked out of the gym in disgust.

Cognitive dissonance, and a heavy dose of it, had clearly taken over. He had talked himself into believing that he could suddenly become a super ballplayer. But why? Pondering this, Wachtler admits candidly, "My desire to prove myself had overcome my reason." Indeed it had, just as his desire to regain Joy Silverman's affections had blinded him to the unrealistic nature of his plan and the high risks it posed for him.

Ironically, the former judge's own position represents to many of us, and correctly so, the antithesis of his out-of-court antics. Judges are supposed to be the essence of rational thinking. They cut through the bull and present reasons for their decisions, adroitly balancing all aspects of the cases before them.

The Wachtler case is a textbook example of how people can compartmentalize their lives. Rational in his work, irrational in his personal life. Perhaps, one can argue, the very pressures of having to constantly adhere to rules and reason created a need to vent his emotions in other areas. Wachtler could not do so in his position as judge because that would have meant embarrassment and humiliation in front of his primary reference group, his colleagues. He did not, at one level, wish to overtly damage the career for which he had worked so hard to succeed. But, at another level, his dark desires to have it his way, regardless of the risks and obstacles they posed, caused him to throw caution to the wind.

Did he really think that creating a fictional character who intimidated Joy and from whom he would rescue her, could work? Had he not seen many instances where even smaller lies were exposed and proven to be fraudulent by the police? Surely he had. Wachtler's refusal to face that led to his downfall. What it shows is how the human mind can become hostage to its own deepest needs and, as happened in Milford, delude itself.

And what of Wachtler's contention, supported by psychiatrists who testified on his behalf, that the blame should properly be placed on his manic depressive illness, particularly his manic phases? No doubt it played a role in his acting out, but personality is formed much earlier in life and, as the stories he himself told reveal, he tended to respond emotionally, even impulsively, only to regret his deeds after they got him into trouble.

Besides, it is equally clear that many manic depressives don't behave in the way that Wachtler did. His illness became a contributory factor to the life of a human being who is, as I discovered even more when I interviewed him, very complex. He implicitly acknowledges this when he notes, "I know that I was indeed sick. And I need no psychiatrist to tell me how manic I was when I did what I did—but I still have difficulty fathoming the mystery of how a human mind, my mind, could become so bereft of reason."

Afterwards, with the benefit of hindsight, things always look different. Reflecting on it while incarcerated, his memory jogged by another book about his misdeeds, written by Linda Wolfe, Wachtler asked himself ruefully, "How could my judgment have been so skewed as to blind me to the ruin I was bringing to a career, a profession, and a marriage, all of which I had nurtured for over forty years[?]"

A large part of the answer to that would lie in his family history, his parents, his brother, and his response to the social and economic circumstances in which he was raised, as well as his basic personality structure. Specific conditions can drive people to be ambitious to the point of unwillingness to accept defeat; to single-mindedly seek power, and to abuse it, while at the same time rigidly conforming to social and professional norms. They can also create strong feelings of insecurity.

Wachtler was a child of the Great Depression. Born in 1930, he led an almost itinerant life in his early, formative years. His father was a traveling auctioneer and the family lived in a number of communities while he was a youngster. The stress of moving from place to place and having to make new friends in each locale, as well as leaving others behind, probably took its toll on him. The fact that he was identified by his family as the brilliant one in whom all hopes would reside, while his brother was given the less glamorous role of preparing to take over the family jewelry store, not only affected his self-image, but placed enormous pressure on him to succeed. It is these and other aspects that must be considered if we are to fully understand this case.

In reality, Wachtler's story is similar to those of so many others who have thrown it all away. The difference is really only one of degree, rather than of kind. He has been the subject of two full-length biographies and has penned his autobiography, as well. His successes notwithstanding, he is also an example of how it can be *who* you are, not *what* you are, that matters most.

As to the specifics, there is much to consider here. Mental illness, ambition, circumstances, and his family history all played a part, but his emotional responses were equally critical in determining what happened to him. Here, as in other situations, it's often impossible to isolate one cause. Rather, each must be considered as part of a larger whole. This is true, as well, of the disgraced financier, Bernie Madoff, as we shall soon see.

WHY WE'RE GREEDY

Greed is fueled by desires that are often irrational. The need to achieve them is often so great that we disregard all the signposts of impending doom—warnings by friends, cautionary tales of how others got into trouble, early signs of trouble as we try to get what we want in any way we can. The reasons for greedy behavior can be broken down into the following eight causes:

1. Insatiable need for recognition
2. Unrealistic thinking
3. Lust for profit
4. Desire for power
5. How we were raised
6. Jealousy
7. Romance and sex
8. Access

CRAVING RECOGNITION

The pattern of pushing and praising, then withholding praise, is well known to psychologists. Highly regarded psychologist and therapist Dr. Helen Ishofsky described this type of behavior:

"I had a person who was always trying to please her parents. Every time she did something good her parents praised her. And that worked until they stopped praising her and then she needed to do something really great again."

"What will happen when her parents die?" I asked.

"Impossible to predict," she replied. "The role of praising may fall upon her husband."

Ishofsky cautions that research also shows that people who are made to feel special as children don't necessarily become driven, *What Makes Sammy Run?* types. It depends on how and in what context praise is dispensed.

Whatever the case, people can develop a thirst or a greed for praise and recognition that is insatiable. Such praise can then create an even greater need for it when given, because the pleasure it provides actually whets the appetite for more. For such people, it's never enough, largely because the insecurities that cause it have never been addressed. Consequently, they can be propelled into excessive responses that lead to embarrassment, ridicule, and worse.

Psychologists have been studying this phenomenon for years. They call it "well-being research." It shows that when good things happen to certain types of people it plays only a small role in their happiness. Far more important is their inherited temperament or personality. If you're not a basically happy person, then even the great delight you feel when something really good happens tends to melt away pretty fast.

Say you win a two-week vacation to the French Riviera. You're ecstatic when you hear about it and later while you're there. But if you're a morose type of individual, then you'll be morose four weeks after you return. Many studies of lottery winners have confirmed that they aren't much happier in the long run. Some of them even get into real trouble because they can't adjust to their new-found wealth.

Management psychologists Nancy Leonard and Michael Harvey explored the workplace behavior of perfectionists driven by fear of failure. They found that such people needed constant praise. They tried desperately to obtain approving statements from superiors, obsessively monitored their status on various lists and rankings, and avoided contact with people whom they thought were of lesser rank.

The desire for recognition can increase as people's ability to perform or produce begins to decline. Who knows exactly what Stephen Ambrose or Doris Kearns Goodwin were thinking when they reportedly plagiarized after reaching the heights of success? Maybe they felt their ideas were becoming stale and so they succumbed to the temptations of borrowing from the writings of others.

They weren't the first to do that and they won't be the last. Another case in point is the almost stereotypical aging Hollywood actor or actress. He or she finds himself or herself in less demand as the years go by. Longer periods of time begin to elapse before they are again given a major part in a film. Or they are reduced to bit parts, roles they would have spurned years ago, but are now forced to take. Instead of accepting this as a normal part of the aging process, they may resort to binge drinking, reckless driving, or frequent blowups with spouses and friends. Afterwards, they regret their behavior, seeing it as foolish or impulsive.

Over-the-hill athletes and fashion models, older corporate executives, mathematicians and professional chess players past their prime—the list is endless, but the syndrome is depressingly familiar. They are people used to the psychic rewards of success who are now unable to accept a diminution in their powers and the decreasing rewards that accompany this stage in their lives.

WHEN YOUR REACH EXCEEDS YOUR GRASP

If you're a greedy type, then it's easy to overreach. In part this can explain why Bernie Madoff paid no heed to the risks he was taking. Anyone in finance, and most people in general, know that Ponzi schemes all fail ultimately. But the longer he got away with it, in his case for decades, the more invulnerable he must have felt.

Highly regarded New York State Nassau County judge Gary Knobel has seen a lot of dumb things in his day. I spoke with him in his chambers about the nature of greed. He's a rare breed of judge—no nonsense, but a lot of compassion for those who come before him:

"I've seen greed cause people to do stupid things. You have lawyers who get a $50,000 settlement offer and it's a good deal under the circumstances. Yet they decide to go to trial and then they lose at the trial stage."

"Do you think the fact that they got the $50,000 makes them think that obtaining the, say, $100,000 might also be possible?" I ask him.

Knobel smiles faintly before responding. Perhaps he's recalling a specific case that came before him. "They think that if the defendant has offered $50,000 then they could probably get even more from the jury. They refuse to believe the reality of the risks they're taking. Namely, you could have a group of strangers who may not like the plaintiff or who may not think your case is good. Or they might have something against the lawyers, the way they speak or look. There are so many factors that go into a jury decision. And the lawyers simply ignore this and roll the dice. I'm talking about a fair offer, of course."

"Why do they do it? After all, they have experience with these situations."

"Because they think they can be big winners."

"So why are you so amazed at this?"

"I'm always amazed that, with their experience in the court system, as you say, the lawyers would be willing to take the chance. And, in most cases, I believe it's pure unvarnished greed. Invariably, those who follow this route end up losing, big time, even if they have a good case. Because you can't ever know for sure what a jury is going to do." What's really happening in such instances is that the initial accomplishment, namely the $50,000 settlement offer, inspires self-confidence. That feeling in itself creates a belief in some people that they can do even better. Until the settlement was offered they had doubts, but once it was, it made them feel that their opponent must be in a weak position. If not, why would he have offered to settle instead of going ahead with a trial?

The lawyers conveniently ignore all the considerations that could have weighed on their opponent—risk of losing, unpredictability of juries, and so on—in short, the same concerns they themselves had initially. They may also be persuaded that their cause was right. And the belief that one is in the right can also lead to greater risk-taking.

A friend of mine in his early forties had a serious back operation. The doctors shaved down the bone that was pressing on a nerve. Don was lucky and the operation was successful. Now he wanted to get back to playing tennis, a game he loved and had been forced to give up. To celebrate the operation's positive outcome and, in effect, to prove to himself and to others how successful it was, he played five straight sets of tennis, two of them doubles, and three of them singles. Afterward he felt sore but basically okay even as he knew he had pushed himself too far too soon.

A few days later I played singles against him in a tournament, unaware of how much he had played in the days preceding the match. Don played badly and lost, but worse than that, his back was really hurting him as we walked off the court. He sat down heavily in a chair off to the side, his face contorted in pain. A minute later he was on his cell phone. "Doc, it's me, Don. Can you give me some pain killers? I need 'em right away. My back's killing me." He subsequently went into spasm for a week.

Why did he risk so much after what he went through? Bad judgment and, most likely, a touch of greed. He wanted it all—to be young and fit again. Don is 42. When I asked him about his decision to play so much so soon, his response was, "I guess I'm not psychologically ready or willing at this age to go down a level in my game. But I'll admit that I should have been smarter and stopped playing when I had the first twinge of pain." He's not the first or last alpha male to feel that way.

THE BLINDING LUST FOR PROFITS

"Writer's Work in *USA Today* is Called False," blared the front page headline in *The New York Times*. This wasn't anything new. Plagiarism has been around for a long time and by 2004, when the story appeared, it was becoming almost routine. What made it different was the scope and the sheer gall exhibited by the well-known reporter, Jack Kelley.

Among his most grievous sins were inventing a personal meeting he supposedly had in Jerusalem with a suicide bomber and claiming he was personally hunting for Osama Bin Laden, not to mention the existence of more than twenty sentences lifted without attribution from stories that appeared elsewhere. *USA Today* dismissed him.

At least he had a vivid imagination. In the Jerusalem story about the bombing of the Sbarro pizza shop, he wrote, "Three men, who had been eating pizza inside, were catapulted out of the chairs they had been sitting on. When they hit the ground their heads separated from their bodies and rolled down the street." It didn't quite happen that way as no one was reported to have been decapitated in the attack, horrifying as it was.

What caught my eye, however, was a quote from Debbie Howlett, *USA Today*'s midwestern correspondent, who expressed anger that no senior people at *USA Today* had admitted any culpability in what Kelley had done. And why were they culpable, in Howlett's opinion? Because, as she put it: "Yes, Jack fabricated many, many stories. But he was aided and abetted by editors who were hungry for prizes and weren't nearly skeptical enough of these fantastical tales." Her criticism was right on point. *USA Today* nominated Kelley for the Pulitzer Prize given for beat reporting. And the phony pizza shop-bombing story was one of nine they submitted to the committee in support of that nomination.

Whatever Kelley's motives for making up stories—desire for fame, power, wealth—it was the greed of newspapers, often driven by financial pressures, that played a prominent role. The not so hidden message sent to reporters is that there's a bottom line approach that reigns supreme—prestigious prizes, circulation numbers, and advertising revenues—that drives the engine of the publishing industry. This is reinforced when reporters who cut corners are given an implicit green light by the failure of editors to hold them accountable to high standards. And when other journalists witness this and the recognition accorded such frauds, they are sorely tempted to follow suit.

This all goes back to the influence of culture on our society, one with demands that encourage and reward greed. It's everywhere. Greed is what caused Bernie Madoff's clients to look the other way even when their high returns made no sense. They *wanted* to believe that those returns were plausible and so they asked no questions.

Doctors are encouraged by profit-hungry HMOs to do as many procedures and tests as they can get away with; plumbers, carpenters, and roofers are encouraged by their bosses to do as many repairs as possible and to charge as much as they can get away with. And when the bill is covered by an insurance company, then it's literally open season as both the customer and the repair-person conspire to inflate the costs. Ditto for selling unhealthy products, damaging the environment, and overcharging for fixing your car. In short, wide segments of our society have been thoroughly socialized into the view that profits are the goal and anything is justified to achieve them. The only difference seems to be between those who think it's okay to be a pig about it and those who believe it's all right as long as you're not a pig about it.

THE LIMITLESS DESIRE FOR POWER

Like money and fame, power plays a major role in greed. Sol Wachtler, the former New York State chief judge, claimed that his psychological problems were the main reason for his bizarre behavior. Yet, even he admitted that his desire for power was an important motivator. In his autobiography, he touches on former Missouri senator Thomas Eagleton and how his career was wrecked by his admission that he'd been hospitalized for depression. Wachtler feared that a similar acknowledgement of mental illness would ruin his own chances for higher office.

Reading his book, the feeling of loss of opportunity becomes readily apparent. Power and respect were among the most important goals for him. Moreover, he realized that mental issues cannot be held solely responsible for what he did, for even the mentally ill have choices in what they do: "Had my most recent manic focus been on positive goals rather than on destructive aberration," he says regretfully, "I might be writing entries from the governor's mansion rather than a prison cell." That sentence says it all.

There are, in fact, many cases where people do run for public office or allow their names to be presented for important posts despite questions about their backgrounds. Then, as they go through the vetting process, skeletons are unearthed. They lied about their degrees, they were arrested, they used drugs, they were implicated in financial scandals. Why didn't they disclose it? Didn't they know it would be found out? Yes, in most instances they did. But their lust for power was so great that they decided to take a chance, hoping the truth would never emerge. And then they looked stupid as their names were withdrawn and their careers derailed. These are not necessarily evil people, or at least not evil in every way. They are people with a major blind spot, an outsized ambition that affects their judgment.

People can also become greedy because of feelings of entitlement. I know a woman whose husband became director of a Little League division in her community. Their son was a so-so pitcher with a medium-speed fastball and a curveball that rarely, if ever, curved. "Timmy is going to be the starting pitcher now," she crowed to me. "We deserve it after all these years, now that Jim's heading the league and doing all this volunteer work." Notice the reference to "we deserve it" as opposed to "he." It's not about their kid even. It's really about them. Those familiar with Little League know well how common this attitude is. Not surprisingly, Jim was soon pursuing another goal—running the Little League at the county level. And then after that, who knows? Maybe Williamsport, Pennsylvania.

HOW WE WERE RAISED

A key factor that determines whether or not people will become greedy is how they were raised. One of Dr. Ishofsky's specialties is treating children whose parents were traumatized. "When that happens," she pointed out, "the children may cross a line because they so badly want to do something which will take their parents' pain away, that will make them feel better. What distinguishes those who don't cross that line from those who do," she continued, "is that their parents have taught them what's acceptable behavior and what's not. They know the rules of the game. You don't do anything embarrassing, or illegal. Not because you're going to get caught, but because it's not the right thing to do."

But trauma is a relative matter. Andrew Kirtzman has written a book about Bernie Madoff, the man who perpetrated one of the biggest financial frauds in history, perhaps *the* biggest. Titled, *Betrayal: The Life and Lies of Bernie Madoff*, it is based on over one hundred interviews with people from his past and on thousands of pages of court testimony, phone conversation transcripts, private e-mails, and the like.

He concludes that one of the major causes of Madoff's scandalous behavior was an adolescence that included rejection by girls whose affections he sought and a mediocre academic record that relegated him to second rate cliques, classes, and schools. Unlike most of his upwardly striving classmates in the then mostly Jewish neighborhood of Laurelton, Queens, Madoff went to a low-ranked school, the University of Alabama, before switching to Hofstra, where he compiled an unimpressive academic record. As a result, he developed a great need to prove himself the equal of his peers. His route was the financial one because if there was an area he excelled in that was it.

The problem with this argument is that Madoff didn't appear to have suffered enough for this to be a major cause. He was, as Kirtzman himself notes, not bullied and not a loner. In fact, he's described as "a fairly popular kid." He could even "shoot a hoop and swim a decent lap." Moreover, he and a friend founded a clique focused on being cool. In short, there's not enough compelling stuff that could explain how a man can scam people he's been friends with for decades, not to mention his sister, out of hundreds of millions of dollars and not give a damn about them. He even bilked the Holocaust survivor and Nobel

Laureate, Elie Wiesel out of all his money. For a Jew to bankrupt Elie Wiesel is like a Catholic robbing a cardinal or an archbishop!

There is one aspect of his early life that does matter, perhaps. His parents operated a stock company from out of their home that ran afoul of the law. While in college, Bernie joined his Dad in illegally trading stocks, and so one could argue that a road map existed for the future. But even that explanation falls short. The truth is that, Madoff was and is a sociopath, a man with no scruples or conscience whatsoever. More on this later.

HOW'S MY NEIGHBOR DOING?

Status is a relative sort of thing. If you're driving a new Audi, it's somehow not as big a deal if everyone else has a car that costs just as much. We tend to measure our success in terms of how everyone else in our social circle is doing. So when we feel that others around us are doing better, it can lead to jealousy. And the need to deal with that emotion can in turn lead to greed as we try to show we're just as good, just as smart, and just as rich as the other person.

It's not a question of ambition. Someone can say, "I live in an apartment and I'd like to live in a house." That's fine, because it's not born out of envy. But if a person says, "I want a house because *John* has a house," that's jealousy and jealousy can lead to poor decision-making. There are people who are worth millions, and yet they're miserable because others are worth millions more.

Two Harvard sociologists, Glenn Firebaugh and Laura Tach, studied how people looked at happiness and making money and concluded that Americans determine happiness mainly by seeing how their income compares to that of others.

Larry Colmer lived in Forest Hills, a middle class community in Queens, New York. He was a teacher in the public school system, making a decent salary. By a quirk of geography, his children attended a public school located in nearby Forest Hills Gardens, a much wealthier community with homes that cost, on average, 2 to 3 million dollars. Sometimes his kids would be invited for play dates to children who lived in these homes. Larry would pick up his two boys and it was right in his face. He couldn't help but notice the disparity.

"It's so unfair," he thought. Why should these people have so much more? He worked just as hard, he reasoned, what with the summers spent selling clothing in his brother's business. "How do you get so rich?" he asked his wife.

"I don't know," she said. "Maybe you're just born with money, or you get lucky in the stock market." Caroline wasn't too interested in the question because she wasn't the jealous type. She was happy with what she had. As for Larry, the feelings of envy wouldn't go away, especially because his kids were asking him questions like, "Why can't we have one of those movie screen TVs? How come we can't go to Italy for Easter vacation? How come Billy and Janet get to go to overnight camp in Maine, while we have to go to a crummy day camp?" It was enough to make him sick.

Larry resolved to do something about it instead of just feeling bad. He took his life savings and, over the protests of his more cautious wife, put them into a small fitness center in Brooklyn. He also persuaded a childhood friend to go in with him. The friend worked days and Larry was there in the evening. The work was hard, but he loved it. He felt he now had a purpose in life. "This will make Forest Hills Gardens," he bragged to his wife.

But things don't always work out the way you plan them. One unexpected development was his sudden attraction to a vivacious woman who worked out regularly in the gym. Pretty soon they were having an affair. The pressures of juggling his teaching job, running the gym, and keeping the woman happy were ultimately too much for him to handle.

Something had to give. He was faced with the choice of either ending the relationship or selling the business, which at that point was only turning a small profit. But his greed wouldn't let him give anything up. So he kept the business and the woman. It ended badly. The fitness center went under and his wife found out about the affair he was having. Two years later, he was divorced, living in a studio apartment in the even more modest neighborhood of Woodside, Queens, and pretty close to broke. Needless to say, he wasn't going to "make Forest Hills Gardens." What killed it for him, in essence, was envy and the desire to "have it all," or his greed.

Sometimes you want to have something so much that you talk yourself into the idea that you can achieve it when really you can't. For instance, you want to be acclaimed as a great writer, but you aren't talented enough to be in that elite class of novelists. So you start paraphrasing a bit here, a bit there and, before you know it, you're actually quoting from other authors. And then you are "discovered," not as a great writer, but as a fraud, a thief of other people's ideas. And what caused it? Your lack of ability, coupled with an intense desire to overcome it. When we refuse to accept our limitations, it's often a set-up for disaster.

INTENSE DESIRE FOR HAPPINESS

Emotions are one of the most frequent obstacles to common sense. People who are prisoners of their emotions lack what the noted author and psychologist Daniel Goleman has called "emotional intelligence." Money, power, fame, and sex are all temptations and gratifications that can stoke the fires of desire, rage, and frustration in people and lead them to grievous miscalculation.

The wish to be happy can be so great that it makes the person oblivious to everything and everyone around them. Alice was a very pretty woman with a successful career. But there was one area where success had eluded her—marriage. After a bitter divorce, she found herself single, with two small children to care for. In her early thirties and aware of the unfavorable ratio of single men to single women in her community, she made strenuous efforts to remarry. She felt an urgent need to find someone soon.

And she did. She met and fell in love with a handsome and wealthy man. He proposed, and she gratefully accepted. The only problem was, she was the only one who thought it was a good idea. "Don't do it, you'll be sorry," her friends told her, all to no avail. She ignored the whispers about her prospective mate. Not only was he a heavy drinker, they warned, but he was neglectful and had been abusive to his previous wife.

The marriage ended six months after the wedding.

"Why didn't you listen to us?" her friends said.

"Why didn't you tell me? I had no idea," she responded.

"We did," they answered, telling her exactly when, where, and what they'd said about Carl.

Alice was most probably telling the truth. She may have heard what they said, but being in no mood to listen, she ignored them and convinced herself they hadn't really said it. People do it all the time. Why did she make such a foolish decision? Because her desire for a husband was so great that she considered being married more important than *whom* she would marry.

A Boston doctor met a woman. A relationship began, the sex was great, and he became totally infatuated with her. Newly single after a nasty divorce, the doctor wanted to move in with her. But how to convince her? Well, she had a cocaine habit and her dealer had just been arrested. The physician decided to go to an area of Roxbury where coke was reportedly widely available. The problem was the cops also knew that and our doctor friend was pulled over.

Asked what he was doing in the neighborhood, he claimed he'd gotten lost. Luckily for him, the cop let him go. Later, reflecting on the incident to me, he said, "I must have been out of my mind to risk everything for her. I mean, buying drugs in bad neighborhoods isn't exactly my field of expertise. But I really loved her and thought I'd impress her by doing it. It's a miracle I wasn't searched and arrested for possession. In the end, she broke up with me anyway, so what was the point of taking such a chance?" Regardless of the outcome, it was a dumb move because the risk far exceeded the, by no means certain, gain.

CRIMES OF OPPORTUNITY

We hear a lot about crimes of opportunity. Sometimes the hand-maiden to greed may be access. Together they fuel the temptation that has existed in all humans since the days of Adam and Eve. No group is more prone to this than politicians. Here you have a class of people who are not especially well paid. Yet they wield enormous power. They can approve programs worth millions of dollars that benefit schools, the elderly, the sick, women, physicians, you name it. They can pass legislation that brings in untold millions of dollars to industry and to corporations.

But they can't have *any* of it, at least not legally. They see all this money changing hands, they witness businessmen and lawyers raking in huge profits, in part because of the laws *they* pass and the programs *they* pass, and they have to make do with their relatively small salary. It's an open invitation to corruption.

We are always being told about greedy politicians. But to what extent has society caused such greed? How are politicians supposed to feel under the circumstances? Let's face it. Their temptations are greater than the ones most of us face. So when they're offered bribes to help this one or that one, they accept and rationalize that this is their due for what they do. This is especially so because our society *expects* politicians to be crooks. For many people, the words "politician" and "crook" are virtually synonymous.

What's the solution? One possibility is to dramatically increase politicians' salaries, to compensate them in such a way that they won't feel so tempted. But won't greedy people always be greedy? Haven't we already said that, for certain people, it's never enough? True, but not for everyone. Different folks have differing satisfaction thresholds and raising salaries will probably prevent enough corruption to make it worthwhile. For such people, the simplest antidote to greed is already having what you need.

4

JUSTICE AND HONOR

"No other club could afford to give the amount the Yankees have paid for him, and I do not mind saying I think they are taking a gamble." Who was this man talking about? Roger Clemens? Alex Rodriguez? Mariano Rivera? It was Babe Ruth, perhaps the greatest player known to baseball.

The speaker, in 1920, was Harry Frazee, then-owner of the Boston Red Sox. Ruth went on to belt 659 homers for the Yankees, sixty in one year. The so-called "curse of the Bambino" (one of Ruth's nicknames) haunted the Sox for the next eighty-six years until they finally won the World Series in 2004. In retrospect, trading Ruth looks like incredibly bad judgment, to say the least. Sure, Frazee, a failed theatrical producer, had his reasons. Ruth was unquestionably a star on a very mediocre team. But he was also a drunk and wanted a lot of money. In Frazee's eyes that made him an expensive showboat who was challenging his authority. Blinded by his own perception of principle and honor, he felt he had to get rid of him even though he was an outstanding athlete.

The relationship between honor and making costly errors is complex and has many aspects to it. I've broken it down here into eleven elements that come into play. There may be others, but these are the most common:

1. Emotional reaction to true injustice
2. Need to be in control
3. Road rage
4. Authority issues
5. Protecting what's yours
6. A sense of dignity
7. What will everybody think?
8. Helping others
9. A need to "get even"
10. Misplaced sense of honor
11. Lies

EMOTIONS AND INJUSTICE

"It's not fair," Johnny says to his mother. "A couple of kids were making jokes and she punished the whole class." A few people in a suburban hamlet fail to pick up after their dogs and an ordinance is passed banning all dogs from a local park. "No fair," cry those who have faithfully used their pooper-scoopers, all to no avail.

These examples are both mild, but no less valid, versions of how people feel when their honor is violated. There is a belief here that the person is not being treated fairly, that there's no justice. It seems, in the individual's view, that the collective punishment being meted out ignores the fact that they are personally blameless. Thus, ultimately, what it comes down to is that they are being "disrespected," not being dealt with honorably.

I was reminded of the salience of this issue one January night when my neighbor's alarm went off at 4:00 a.m. They had gone to Florida on vacation and neglected to leave a key with anyone else. The alarm wailed away for two days and nights, angering everyone within ear-shot. The police came and told us that the alarm company had only the young couples' parents' number. As it turned out, Mom and Dad and their key to the kids' house were all 1,500 miles away in the Sunshine State. How unfair and inconsiderate, the neighbors thought, their anger fueled by images of the family lying on a lovely beach in the warm sun, while the rest of us had to contend with a New York winter.

"What can we do about it?" one neighbor asked the cop. "The alarm's gone off eight or nine times. We've already dialed their parents' home number twice and left messages."

"You can file a formal complaint and sign it. Once you do that, we call emergency services and they come and cut the wires."

"And then, when the people come back, they just put the wires back?"

The officer cleared his throat nervously and gave us a wary look, as if we were all legal eagles trying to trip him up. "It's not always that simple. The alarm company can charge the owners an arm and a leg. And then the neighbors can turn around and sue you. I've seen it happen. You got nice neighbors and you got nasty neighbors. You wanna be careful with people who live next door to you. I remember a case where some people got pissed at this guy on their block because he'd complained about noise. To get him back they kept reporting him to the village about his lawn, that he hadn't cut the grass down far enough. And they had the fellow in the municipal court five or six times, and he's a guy in his nineties."

My wife and I were acquainted with the couple, who were in their early thirties. We didn't think what they did was inconsiderate, but rather a result of their youth and inexperience as homeowners. So we decided to go the last mile. We made a few more calls, got hold of the realtor who sold them the home, and she gave us the mother's cell phone number. When we finally reached them in Florida, the young man was very apologetic and said he would FedEx the key and the alarm code to us so we could disable the system. The other neighbors also realized that the couple's failure to leave a key was not malicious, though one of them did describe it as "irresponsible." What had really bothered them was that the couple wasn't there to see how loud and annoying the sound of the alarm going off had been. That, compounded with their knowledge that the couple was enjoying a vacation when they weren't, contributed to a feeling that it somehow wasn't fair or just.

When something like this happens people can have difficulty exercising restraint as they know they should. You try to put money in the meter and it's broken, but the "fail" sign is not working. It just takes your coins and reads "expired." Free parking is available two blocks away, but you're right in front of the restaurant you're going to, so why should you have to pay the price for the city's malfunctioning meters? Well, it turns out you do have to pay the price, because you get a thirty-five dollar ticket and don't have the time or inclination to fight it. Parking there was clearly a bad decision, but your overdeveloped sense of justice kicked in and that was that.

Here's another situation that many people have been in. The light seems to be taking forever to change. You're sitting in your car, waiting. The driver ahead of you decides that it's been long enough and inches forward, sort of sliding through the intersection. "Okay," you say. "If he can do it, so can I," as if the other driver just gave you permission. Too bad he's not the one who gives permission. No sooner do you go through the light than you are stopped by a passing patrol car. To make matters worse, the light changes just at that moment. "But the guy ahead of me also went through it," you protest to the officer. "Maybe, but you're the guy I saw," he says unsympathetically. That's what people mean when they use the hackneyed expression, "Life isn't fair."

You are delayed by a toll collector who is short of change and must go to another booth to get it. This takes five minutes away from a very tight schedule. You speed away and continue speeding, rationalizing that you wouldn't have had to drive so fast, had the toll collector not been short of change. Therefore, it's his fault. Alas, you are caught in a radar trap and fined for speeding. Needless to say, the judge does not accept your explanation and you receive a hefty fine.

One final story before we move on. A fellow commuter told me the following tale of woe: He tried to buy a train ticket in advance from a machine. He inserted the money but the machine refused to accept it. He tried three other machines, all with the same result, by which time he had to board the train. As he sat there, he thought about the injustice of it. After all, it was the railroad's responsibility to maintain their equipment, not his. Yet he knew the conductor would almost surely reject this excuse and make him pay eighteen dollars for an on-train purchase instead of the nine-dollar advance price.

The more he thought about it the madder he got and he finally resolved not to pay it, no matter what. At the next stop, before the conductor came by his seat, he jumped off the train for a second and then reboarded. When the conductor came by a moment later, he said he had just gotten on, which, if it were true, would have only cost him ten dollars. "You're lying," the conductor said. "I saw what you did." He was pulled off at the next major stop, taken to the stationmaster, and fined for fare evasion.

All of these vignettes involve events beyond one's control. In each case a sense of injustice stirs righteous anger. That emotion clouds one's judgment. You're a normally law-abiding citizen, but not when you feel unfairly treated. In each instance, had you thought it through calmly, you would have decided that the risk far outweighed the gain. Adding to the problem is that you feel you *shouldn't* have been caught because you were in the right. Unfortunately, that has nothing to do with whether or not you'll be caught.

A NEED TO BE IN CONTROL

Anger can stem from a need to be in control, to look strong. This can lead to serious lapses in judgment. One businessman I know ruefully told me how he blew a big deal, worth millions, because of it. He had met with a man and discussed buying a piece of property from him. The seller promised to call within a day and didn't do so for a week, most likely figuring that this would provoke anxiety in the other party and soften him up. But the buyer felt that he was being disrespected. When the seller finally called him after a week to discuss and negotiate the price, he was shocked when the man, who was by now infuriated, called off the deal. "You're not in charge here!" he screamed into the phone. "I am. I'm the buyer, so to hell with you! Keep your goddamn property!"

His last words told the story. He wanted to be respected and he wanted to be in control. A week later, he deeply regretted the missed opportunity over what he admitted was a clash in value systems. And why are value systems so important to people? Because they anchor, and therefore protect us. They provide us with a road map of how to deal with the world and we compromise on them with great difficulty, or, as was the case here, not at all. Although my friend knew he would lose a great deal of money, he couldn't help himself and made a very bad business decision.

A psychologist told me the following story, one that illustrates how the need to be in control can quickly get out of hand:

> A patient of mine is pulled over on Central Avenue by a female cop for an illegal turn. He's behind in his rent and he's got other problems. And he's with his wife. And she's also a woman who gives him orders. So he starts talking back to the cop. He tells the cop: "I'm calling your precinct. I work for the city and I'm the same as you. I've got the same health insurance." Totally idiotic. The officer grabs the guy's cell phone and she calls for backup. My patient ends up in jail.
>
> It was the stupidest thing in the world. So why did he do it? He said to me, "These cops have an attitude." He's a high school art teacher, a responsible job, but he's being totally irrational even though he's a bright guy. He does have anger management issues and something else had happened that day, at work.

What we also see here is that your mood, related perhaps to other things going on in your life, can exacerbate things. The man was a stereotypical, hen-pecked husband. The fact that the cop was a woman probably didn't help inasmuch as it reminded him of his demanding wife. When he says that they both have the same employer and health insurance, he's trying to imply that they are of equal status and that she therefore shouldn't hassle him. But in this situation, they're not equals. One has the power, the other doesn't. The fact that he's bright is irrelevant because emotions and IQ often don't correlate. His tendency to get angry is obviously a factor but might not have kicked in were it not for the other elements in the case.

ROAD RAGE

The potential for fury that can be unleashed by human beings seems to flourish in what we call road rage. Andrew Burnett got into a fender bender in California and a shouting match ensued with the driver of the other car, a woman with a coincidentally similar name, Sara McBurnett. Burnett lost his temper and suddenly reached into the woman's auto, grabbed her bichon frise, and hurled him into the road where he died after being struck by an oncoming vehicle. What Ms. McBurnett said to Burnett to provoke him is unknown, but he clearly lost his cool. At the sentencing, Burnett said, "I'm really sorry for what happened. If there's anything I could ever say or do to bring Leo back, I would."

Here's an example to which many people can no doubt relate: Let's say someone cuts you off in traffic. You want to punish him by tailgating him or by pretending you're going to hit him, so you cut across two lanes of traffic and in the process, crash into another vehicle. Later, as you lie in a hospital bed with serious injuries, you wonder why you reacted so strongly. And as you ponder that, you realize that had you only had more time to reflect, you wouldn't have driven so recklessly to avenge the perceived invasion of your "space" and "insult" to your pride.

And then we have extreme cases where there is actual loss of human life. Thirty-three-year-old Long Island resident Robert Codosea was stabbed to death in a fight that occurred during an altercation early one morning on the Sunken Meadow State Parkway. What triggered the dispute was unknown—perhaps a challenge to authority, honor, or an insult—but he and another driver, Kenneth O'Keefe, exchanged heated words, climbed out of their cars, and began fighting in the rain.

Major Walter Heesch of the New York State Police best summed up the tragedy when he said, "Here's two people living a normal life, going on their daily normal routine, and they become involved in some kind of vehicular incident, and it escalates to the point where one person dies. It's senseless. It shouldn't happen. It should never happen."

But it did, and it does, all too often in this country. Kenneth O'Keefe, forty-seven years old, worked the night shift at Entenmann's Bakery and was on his way home. Robert Codosea was a mechanic for Suburban Exterminators and was on his way to his job. He left behind three children, ages three, six, and ten. "This was my baby brother," Diego Codosea said. "I still don't believe it."

Road rage is a national problem. Indeed, in a recent Gallup Poll, over 40 percent of respondents identified it as the greatest hazard on the road today. And why not? An estimated *one third* of all fatal crashes are traceable to road rage. The causes of road rage lie within our deepest emotions, for they are a way in which we deal with our anger and frustrations. The fact that we believe we are invulnerable as we sit inside a powerful vehicle gives us the nerve to lash out when we feel that our personal freedom is being violated. But it's all an illusion, for those we attack can harm us, and we can also be incarcerated for our own attacks on others.

The question is, what, besides better law enforcement, can be done about it? One study of such drivers by Seiji Takaku, a professor at

Saka University of America, found that when drivers were forced to focus on their own past wrongdoing as reckless drivers, they were much more apt to forgive those they felt had wronged them on the road. This happened because they realized it was hypocritical to blame others for bad driving, when they were guilty of the same offense. One way to prevent such behavior is to make such awareness part of driver education classes.

AUTHORITY ISSUES

When the wrong people feel their authority is threatened, it can be extremely dangerous. In his book on evil behavior, *Seductions of Crime*, sociologist Jack Katz describes a case where a father beat his five-week-old child to death after he found him crying. The father, he reports, viewed the infant's behavior as deliberate and offensive, a challenge to his parental authority. Katz calls this "righteous slaughter" and points out that if the father was "crazy" he was crazy well before the event, and that, in any case, the behavior was based on his "moral" idea of what was right and wrong.

Nor was the murder committed while he was doing something else wrong, like sexual abuse. He didn't suddenly "explode and kill while irrationally flailing about." And if he were merely trying to "get rid" of an annoying baby, he could have thrown it out the window. Tragically, what's going on here is a horrible extension of a father who feels he must discipline his child whom, he has convinced himself, is bad and must be punished to preserve the honor of parental authority. It is an extreme perversion of the concept of honor.

Such motives play out on a grander scale when nations go to war, with far more horrifying consequences numerically. When matters of national pride are at stake, the affront is often seen as so great that it justifies lashing out both disproportionately and indiscriminately. The country and its leaders want to inflict pain so that the other side feels their own pain. In so doing they hope to insure that the insult is not repeated. And why is that so important? Because the pain for the injured nation is so severe that it doesn't want to ever bear it again.

Thus, in the Middle East, Hezbollah launches rocket attacks against northern Israel despite the fact that what it has done has enormous consequences—a million refugees, thousands dead, billions of dollars in losses. These losses can be to themselves or to related parties. No matter, their honor is at stake. And, of course, it takes Israeli soldiers prisoner for similar reasons.

The Israeli response is equally strong as civilian areas are also bombed. I spent some time interviewing Palestinians in Gaza and Jenin for a documentary film on the Middle East called *Blood and Tears*. There was the usual litany of complaints. Israelis were occupying the land, homes were being destroyed, but the strongest objections were not to what was being done but *how* it was being done. What bothered people the most was mistreatment at the checkpoints, whenever it occurred. They described in vivid detail how they were forced to undress, how their belongings were flung at them, and how they were called names. The Israeli authorities said such actions were the exception, but the point is that, however infrequent, it was what bothered the Palestinians most. It reminded them that they were definitely not in control and that they were weak and powerless.

PROTECTING WHAT'S YOURS

"A man's home is his castle," they say, and so it is. This country has a long tradition of latitude toward citizens who are protecting their home and property. As a result, Americans see their property as an extension of themselves and encroachments on it are viewed as requiring a response, if only as a matter of honor. When African-American John White, whom we've already discussed in chapter 1, confronted a group of white teenagers on his lawn who were threatening him, he saw them as not only a threat but as people who had violated his sense of personal space. He is by no means the first person in the United States to have shot someone who refused to get off his property. His extreme response may have been dumb, but so was that of the teenagers who failed to understand the symbolic meaning of where they stood.

Sometimes people are motivated to act because they fear losing a treasured possession. Katz tells the story of a woman who killed her lover who was about to leave her for someone else. If she could not have him then she would make sure no one else could either. In this way, she takes the high road as she sees it—she preserves a relationship that would otherwise end in her being replaced by someone else, an outcome she could not bear. Thus, their relationship becomes frozen in time, in a very real sense.

A SENSE OF DIGNITY

Honor matters more to some people than to others but it seems to cut across social, economic, and gender lines. Sol Wachtler writes engagingly about his life in a Butner, South Carolina prison . He was eating a dry, tasteless hamburger, thinking that the best part of the meal was the bag of potato chips that went along with it. Those chips would taste even better at night in his cell, he thought. The only problem was getting them out of the dining room without being spotted by the ever-watchful guards. On impulse, he stuffed them under his sweatshirt. As he put it, "It wasn't that I wanted to get away with anything. It's just that the thought of these potato chips as a midnight snack was overwhelming."

Wachtler continues his story, and here it's actually quite funny: "My surreptitious concealment of the silvery bag was apparently witnessed by everyone in the dining room, especially the guards." Three of them approached him and asked him what was under the sweatshirt. Wachtler pulled it up as if to prove his innocence, and the potato chips came tumbling out. The knot of prisoners who had gathered around and the guards all laughed heartily. After all, it was a minor infraction.

But Wachtler didn't laugh. In his words: "I saw nothing funny about a sixty-four year old former Chief Judge, in prison, caught in the act of filching a bag of potato chips." It's clear that Wachtler had a very strong sense of pride and dignity about who he was, or once was, namely a nationally known judge. The degree to which he felt that way emerges in his introduction to this vignette: "It's a story I'm ashamed to tell—not because I made the effort, but because I made it so pathetically and, in the process, made such a fool of myself." How others perceive people is often of crucial importance to them.

The rich and powerful don't have a monopoly on sensitivity to slights. In truth, it's far more likely to affect the poor. Impassioned murder is far more apt to be committed by low-income people. This is because their already downtrodden state makes it harder for them to deal with assaults on their pride. Conversely, the middle and upper classes have greater opportunities to counter the humiliation that can lead to violence.

In the film *Babel,* a Mexican is stopped at the U.S. border and questioned by the authorities. He cooperates, producing his ID when asked to and answering questions. But the officer suddenly starts screaming at him for no apparent reason. In no time, the Mexican gets upset. "Stop yelling at me," he says repeatedly, to no avail. The officer yells even louder.

It is clear that the driver feels his dignity as a human being is under attack. Suddenly he guns his car and speeds across the border, crashing through several barriers along the way. His passengers, a woman and two small children, suffer greatly because of his precipitous actions.

Could this escalation have been avoided? Definitely. Had the officer not shouted at him, the driver would probably not have done what he did. Thus we see that when a person perceives his honor to be at stake, he may well do something stupid, something he wouldn't ordinarily do. The officer's actions, also not very smart, can be attributed to bad judgment.

In 1971, two young Americans, friends of mine, were touring Istanbul. Some people they met invited them to dinner at a private club. Afterward, members of the group played several games of ping-pong. Anne, a marketing analyst from St. Louis, played against a Turkish man of about twenty. She was a good player and decided to play her best. The result? She won, 21 to 18, at which point her opponent flung his racquet to the ground in frustration. And then he turned to another man who was standing nearby and, for no discernible reason, punched him. Startled, the man socked someone else. Apparently it was a case of mistaken identity—he didn't realize that the man wasn't the one who hit him. Within minutes a full-scale brawl erupted. The police had to be called to restore order.

It seems plausible to assume that the man's frustration stemmed, in part, from the fact that he had not only been beaten by a foreigner, but more significantly for a Muslim, by a woman. His feeling of having been shamed was most probably what brought his anger to a boil.

WHAT WILL EVERYBODY THINK?

Acting to preserve one's honor can depend on whom you are with. When you are alone you can more easily turn the other cheek because no one knows what's happening to you. You hear a noise on a darkened street and begin walking quickly in the opposite direction. But if you're with someone you are apt to feel a greater need to avoid humiliation. This is particularly so if you are in a public place. A good example would be where you've just been bodily tossed out of a nightclub, and passersby are looking at you like you're a criminal of some sort. Feelings of shame are also more intense if it's in front of your family or close friends. Men fighting over a woman's affections is another trigger point.

Sometimes the humiliation is very public indeed. One such case where it may have been responsible for tragedy was that of John F. Kennedy Jr. Clinical psychologist Dr. Steven Luel practices in New York City. Energetic and insightful with an ability to cut to the chase, he gave me his professional take on what happened:

"Here's an example of a guy who crashed his plane and who didn't have enough flying time. He wasn't trained in the instruments he was using. He didn't have the rating."

"Okay," I say. "So it's a dumb move, big time. Why did he do it?"

"Well, first he's got his wife to impress," responds Luel. "And he was thinking he could take risks; he could succeed. 'I'm not a loser.' He's saying to himself, 'I may have had to take the bar exam a couple of times, but eventually I passed it. The *New York Post* is wrong with their headline, 'The Hunk Flunks.' I mean, it's hard to live with that.

"They claimed he also did some cocaine. Anyway, he says, 'I'll figure this out. I know enough about flying planes and I'll get us there.' And, of course, he didn't. I remember it vividly. I often repeat the quote from my father: 'Better to be a live dog than a dead lion.' My father lived by that. And Kennedy definitely didn't have that. His approach was 'Better to be dead than castrated.'"

The belief that you will be embarrassed can also lead you to do things that will prevent embarrassment. An acquaintance of mine bought a motorboat that turned out to be too costly to run. Plus, he thought it was badly designed. The answer was, get rid of it. But he couldn't bear to do that because he'd told everyone whom he knew what a bargain it had been. So he kept it and felt like a fool.

The sociologist Charles Horton Cooley coined an apt term that explains why this happened. He called it "the looking-glass self." When we look in the mirror in the morning, we are technically looking at ourselves. But we really aren't, argues Cooley. When we peer into that mirror, we're really looking to see how we appear to *others* whom we care about or whom we may meet that day.

Sometimes we refer to embarrassment as "losing face," and here's a perfect example of it. You ask your friend to get your nephew a summer job. It doesn't seem like such a big deal, but as it turns out, your pal can't deliver and you get angry. In your mind, it's because she wasn't willing to stick her neck out, but the truth is she simply lacked the necessary connections to get him the job.

Not believing that, you take it to the next level and abruptly end the friendship. "That'll show her," you say to yourself, but in the end, you may be the bigger loser. This friendship had many psychic and real benefits. You went places together, you shared happy occasions, and you even confided in each other. Ironically, that has a good deal to do with why you feel so betrayed. As a result, pride doesn't allow you to take the first step toward reconciliation. And your friend certainly can't take it, because she feels she did nothing wrong. And so a relationship ends over what you eventually come to feel was a silly issue. Why? The passage of time often has a way of making what seemed important at the time, seem less so.

HELPING OTHERS

In matters of honor, other people can sometimes goad you into doing something that you wouldn't ordinarily do. I was telling a friend of mine how a colleague pushed me into complaining about an administrator with whom we were both annoyed. This had resulted in my bearing the brunt of the administrator's anger. "I shouldn't have let him convince me to step out," I said to my friend.

"I know just how you feel," George said. "A similar thing happened to me many years ago and the outcome was much worse. We lived in an apartment complex in Atlanta and there were a bunch of rowdy single guys who lived on the other side of the courtyard. They often had loud, late-night parties that disturbed the rest of the people. Some of us had small children. But everybody was afraid to tangle with them.

"I'm sort of a leader type, as you know, and the other people realized that. So they pushed me to do something about it and finally, I gave in, though I didn't really want to. I mean, who needs the aggravation? Janet [his wife] begged me not to. 'Stay out of it,' she said. 'Let someone else do it.' So I hesitated and talked to the other families. 'We'll go with you,' they said.

"So I went ahead. On the night we were supposed to go over, though, they all chickened out. They didn't give any reason. They just didn't show. Well, I guess I felt I should show some courage, not like those wimps. And so I went to the apartment by myself. They looked at me, I'm not a big guy obviously, and they just laughed. 'Go home and take care of your kids,' they said. 'Don't bother us.'

"When I heard that, I got really mad. 'Don't bother us?' I yelled. *'You're bothering us!'* And then, without any warning, one of these guys belted me, right in the jaw. I fell down and they start kicking me. I was trying to get up so I could get away from them, when one of them grabbed me by my shirt, pulled me up, opened the door and just shoved me out.

"I came home, I wasn't hurt bad, but I looked like a mess. My wife took one look at me and started crying. 'I told you not to be a hero. Sure, the others will tell you to fight, but you're the one who's paying the price.'"

"What did you do then?" I asked. "What finally happened?"

"Well, I was going to go to the police, but then I thought the better of it. I mean, these animals knew where I lived, so, you know the saying, 'Discretion is the better part of valor.' I let it go. Luckily, they moved out a couple of months later. But I learned a lesson. Don't try to be a hero."

Many times people don't have to be goaded into action. This is because they're doing something for someone else for altruistic reasons.

In one rather bizarre case, William Barrington-Coupe, a sound engineer, passed off recordings by other famous pianists as belonging to his wife, also a pianist, but not especially well known. His only goal was to win recognition for her, which he felt had been denied her due to her poor health.

Music critics raved about her work, but eventually his deception was discovered. Her husband voiced regret over his actions. Since he gained nothing tangible from what he did, it was a case of wanting to give someone you love a place in the sun.

A NEED TO GET EVEN

The admonition, "don't cut off your nose to spite your face," has become trite, like so many sayings, because there's a good amount of truth in it. We usually employ it when we're telling people, or ourselves, that something's not worth the hassle. The following tale is an excellent illustration of this:

Doris Morton owns a boutique near where I live. I was shopping for a gift there one day and we got into a discussion about repairmen who don't do what they're supposed to do. Doris is in her late forties and has an air of self-confidence, almost bordering on cockiness. She's a pretty tough cookie, in my estimation.

"I don't stand for it," I opined, knowing she'd agree.

"I don't either," she replied, "but sometimes it can be more trouble than it's worth."

"I'm surprised you'd say that. What do you mean?" I asked her.

"Well, I'm not saying I don't fight back, but sometimes winning isn't everything. Let me tell you what I mean, so you'll understand: I hired a plumber about two years ago to do a job in my house. The cost came to about $2,000. Then, after I'd given him the check, I discovered a minor problem with some washers that were no good. I called them up and asked them to come back and fix it.

'They're on a big commercial job now, and they don't have any free time. They'll get to it, probably in about three to four weeks,' was the answer I got.

'But I need it now. My faucets are leaking. It'll only take a few minutes once they get here.'

'Then get another plumber,' the woman in their office said.

"When I heard that I started to get mad. 'Why should I have to pay someone else extra? You screwed this up. It's your obligation to fix it, not mine.' I cursed her out, and she cursed me back and hung up on me. Two minutes later I get a call from the plumber himself. So I start to tell my story.

"He interrupts me after about a minute and says: 'Lady, get yourself an attorney if you don't like it. And a psychiatrist too, while you're at it. You're harassing me.'

"I was furious and I made up my mind to take the guy to court. It was only about seventy-five dollars worth of repairs, but I was outraged. How dare he treat me, or anyone else for that matter, this way? I was hell bent on making him pay in other ways, on *punishing* him. I figured he'll lose time, have to show up in court, and maybe lose too. Well, to make a long a story short, I did win. He had to pay me the seventy-five dollars. But because he kept getting postponements, it took three appearances, and when you added up everything, it was ten hours out of my life. Was it worth it just to save my self-respect? You tell me."

A MISPLACED SENSE OF HONOR

One of the cruelest things you can do is program someone for failure. You are a successful businessman and you want your son to succeed you. You "groom" him to take over, but he's not capable and your employees know it. He may not have the management skills or financial acumen. He may simply not be interested. He doesn't directly tell you any of these things, he just fails. The business and everyone in it suffers.

Lionel Brenner, an acquaintance of mine, was such a person. He grew up in Los Angeles where his father, Jack, headed a midsize coffee distribution company with about sixty employees. Since his older brother decided to become a dentist, Lionel was ultimately tapped to become the CEO.

But Lionel wasn't suited for this type of work. He liked music, the theater, and films. His father chose to ignore reality, pleading with his son, "The Brenners have been in this business for three generations. You can't just leave it. My grandfather would turn over in his grave. Don't do it to me. It'll break my heart." In the end, Lionel, a passive man but one with a great deal of family loyalty, gave in to Dad and stayed.

That turned out to be a fatal error. With other companies encroaching on his territory and luring away his clients, the business began to fail. Lionel's loyalty, or sense of honor, had prevented him from making the right decision. He just couldn't bear the thought of disappointing his ailing father. He had nightmares about his father dying a broken man and blaming him. In the end, the company went under. Good intentions can never replace hard reality.

People often say, "Swallow your pride," but for many it's just too much to swallow. This is especially so when they feel others are depending on them or looking up to them. In the 1970s, I was teaching sociology at Yale. A young black man from Detroit was in my class. Tall and slender with wire-rimmed glasses that gave him a somewhat owlish appearance, he seemed to be having great difficulty with the work. He would ask me to repeat things in class. Then, afterward, he would wait until everyone had left and come up and ask me to repeat the points once more. Despite the time I spent explaining the material, it just didn't seem to sink in. He was failing the biweekly quizzes and clearly couldn't keep up.

I asked him to come by and see me. A product of the sixties, I had great sympathy for minority students and wanted him to do well. At twenty-seven, I wasn't much older than him and could personally identify with what college students go through. Affirmative action was in its infancy then and there were very few black students at Yale. He sank down in the chair I offered him, his shoulders slumped forward.

"What's wrong?" I asked him.

"Nothing," he said softly, without any conviction in his voice.

"Look, Francis, I know you're having trouble with the class. That's quite evident. But I want to help you. How are you doing in your other classes?" He looked up and gave me a searching look. I saw the pain he was feeling.

"To tell you the truth, I'm doing terribly. This isn't the only class I'm having problems with, professor. I don't belong here. I can't understand most of what's being said in class. I feel like such a failure."

"If you don't belong here," I asked gently, "then how come you're here? You obviously had to do well to get in."

"'Well' is a relative term," he said bitterly. "Yeah, I was the valedictorian of my class, but it was an inner city school and the standards were pretty low. My A's would have probably been C's in a regular school. Yale came by and they were looking for good black students. The college counselor recommended me. He said that even though my SATs weren't that good, I was a really hard worker and would do well. It was hard to find qualified minority students then and so they accepted me.

"The fact is, I was scared to go. I didn't have the confidence. I'd grown up poor, in a bad neighborhood, and most of my friends weren't even going to college. Where I came from it was a big deal to even finish high school."

Having done my doctoral dissertation and first book on a branch of the Black Panthers, I knew he spoke the truth. "If you were scared to go, what made you decide to go?"

"I had no choice! Absolutely no choice!" he exclaimed angrily. And then, tears forming in his eyes, his voice breaking, he said, "They made me a party at the high school. My parents came, my relatives came, *everybody* came, even the pastor of my church. I became a local celebrity. 'Francis is a genius,' they said."

I looked at a point on the wall, somewhere behind his head. I didn't know what to say. Should I tell him to work harder, to get counseling? It seemed that the problem went way beyond that. In my heart I knew he couldn't make it without massive help. As I thought about it, he continued:

"Now I can't go back. I'd be too ashamed. How can I face those people and admit that I'm a failure? But I can't stay either. Maybe I'll just say I didn't like it and switch to an easier school. I don't know what to do. Sometimes I just feel like killing myself. But don't worry, I won't. I'm just talking. Still, it hurts so much. I shouldn't have allowed myself to be pushed into it. I feel like I was set up."

In a way he was. Expectations and hopes had been raised. He had come to represent the dreams of his family, school, and community. Although he was unsure of his ability to make it, how could he dash those hopes? And to Yale, no less! A place most white kids couldn't get into, he thought.

The university, like other elite colleges, was desperate to admit minority students. That was the government mandate. They might have engaged in wishful thinking, a little cognitive dissonance perhaps, when they convinced themselves that despite his combined 1170 score on the SATs, he could still do it.

In the end, when we consider the shame and humiliation such students experience and their sense of failure, we do them a great disservice. Though the dynamics and backgrounds may not be the same, it's really no different than a student who comes from money and is admitted to a university way above his abilities because Mommy and Daddy gave money for a building on campus. He goes, does poorly, smokes pot all day, and cracks his car up on a highway and is severely injured. But at least he has the safety net of money and influence to cushion the blow when he leaves.

Francis wasn't the only minority student to suffer this fate. But, at the same time, not all minority students ended up like him. Ted Washington, another black student, was in that same seminar. He also came from an inner city school as it happened, located in Boston's Dorchester section, but he was far more prepared. He performed brilliantly in the class. His father was a writer and had imbued his son with the importance of reading from an early age. I've never forgotten Ted. A chubby young man, with serious, doe-like eyes and a perpetually curious air about him, he constantly peppered me with questions during the class, not aggressively, just persistently. He would spot contradictions in arguments in a flash. He turned in the best term paper in the seminar, totaling seventy pages. I saved it for posterity and still have it. It reminds me of how important it is not to prejudge or stereotype.

I spoke with an administrator after my frustrating and ultimately disheartening meeting with Francis and she promised to look into it. It was near the end of the semester and I only saw Francis two more times. He did not return the following year and I never found out what happened to him. But I hope he found a way to restore his battered ego and do something with his life. It's one of those situations where you can't blame someone for blaming others for their plight. There was certainly enough to go around.

LIES

Finally, let's see how honor and lying might be interrelated. Clearly we do, at times, tell lies to save our honor. And sometimes we get into trouble when we do. We're at a party and say we've read a book that everyone's talking about and we haven't. Then someone says, "What did you think of it?" and we struggle to respond. But what about those who hear our lies? Can they end up responding in ways that are harmful to themselves? It turns out they can.

One of Dr. Liss-Levenson's specialties is family therapy—divorce, marriage, and relationships with children. She sees connections not apparent to even the most practiced eye and she combines common sense with great knowledge. She is confident in her views and comes up with creative interpretations for seemingly inexplicable behavior. I asked her about lying and what it does to people on the receiving end.

"It can affect lots of things. I've had more than one patient who lied about finishing their degree, including cases where they lied even to their spouses. And often they were close to finishing their BA. When they met the person they were dating and that individual had a college degree, they felt that the person might not have been interested in them unless they had a similar level of education.

"When things got serious, they confessed that they didn't really have the degree. Then the issue became, not that they lacked an education, but that they lied. And the one who was lied to considered ending the relationship."

"Should you always tell the truth?" I asked.

"Telling the truth is generally the best policy, but it's important to pay attention to timing. You don't necessarily want to tell everything about yourself on your first date. Say a person suffers from a particular medical condition. They should reveal that to their date, but again, not necessarily right at the beginning of the relationship. People often say, 'Tell the truth and things will work out.' But it doesn't always 'work out.' Or another way to look at it is that 'work out' doesn't mean that the relationship will continue."

When someone is lied to, they often feel that it means the other person doesn't trust them with the truth. It also means that the other person is, in at least some sense, not really who they say they are. If it's what we call "a white lie," then it usually doesn't matter, but lying about big things does. What makes a relationship special is that people are willing to let their guard down, to not be afraid to reveal who they are and their shortcomings. That takes courage and self-confidence.

But those who are lied to may read too much into it. The other person may be a good human being in many other ways. And, let's not forget, they admitted that they held back but are now telling the truth. Yet some people cannot forgive dishonesty when they are the victims. They feel that as a "matter of principle," they must break off the relationship. Later on, they reflect upon and always wonder about what might have been. But it's too late.

5

THE EASY WAY OUT

M arilee Jones isn't exactly a household name, but when you say, "She's the MIT admissions director who lied on her resume," many people are apt to respond, "Oh yeah, I remember that." I was at a party when the story broke and people were talking about her. I recall one wag remarking, "Well, it just goes to show you—you don't have to have a college degree to do a good job. Wasn't she there a long time?"

There was some truth to the statement, but we are, at the end of the day, a society that believes in credentials. That's why we have colleges in the first place, and medical schools, and a host of training programs that give certificates to their graduates. If nothing else, a college degree means that you started something that required work and some intelligence to complete.

People routinely cover up with what are often called "white lies." They will embellish, leave out key details, or not divulge anything about a given topic. Often it seems like the easy way to do it and, in fact, it is. But sometimes, what looks easy can become rather messy, as in the case of Jones. You dissemble and then a new complication emerges. Someone from your past resurfaces, or two people run into you when you're not where you told your wife or husband you'd be. Then you wonder why you lied or why you failed to make amends. Arrayed against simply telling the truth are a host of emotions and temptations that need to be considered if we're to understand this phenomenon:

1. Confessing can be expensive
2. Fame and fortune
3. When opportunity knocks
4. Perceived necessity
5. Almost true
6. Fear
7. Lying is habit-forming
8. Pressure
9. Intolerance for uncertainty
10. The very real complications of coming clean
11. Too much optimism

THE HIGH COST OF CONFESSION

Marilee Jones worked for the Massachusetts Institute of Technology (MIT) Admissions Department for almost three decades, rising to the number one post of dean of admissions before being "outed" by an unnamed individual who contacted a dean at MIT. As it turned out, she was a total fraud. She'd falsely claimed to have degrees from Rensselaer Polytechnic Institute, Union College, and Albany Medical College. Loads of people list phony degrees on their resumes, but few attain such heights in such prestigious schools and last so long to boot. Her resignation statement to the press, reported on April 28, 2007, was appropriately contrite:

"I misrepresented my academic degrees when I first applied to MIT twenty-eight years ago and did not have the courage to correct my resume when I applied for my current job or at any time since. I am deeply sorry for this and for disappointing so many in the MIT community and beyond who supported me, believed in me, and who have given me extraordinary opportunities."

Actually, it's no wonder she "misrepresented" her qualifications. Had she admitted to lying when she applied for the coveted number-one position in the department in 1997, she would never have gotten it. In fact, she probably would have been canned on the spot. Oh yes, it seems she might have a legitimate degree from the College of Saint Rose, a small Catholic institution in Albany. But she never listed it and the college was mum about any details. Even if true, the main sin was listing degrees from other, far more well-known universities and never admitting they were all false.

Normally, we would be left with a trail from childhood that might or might not be revealing—interviews with people who knew her as a kid, as an adult, observations by former colleagues and students, and so on. In this case, however, we have something very unusual, almost unique, to ponder: Long considered an authority on college admissions, Marilee Jones coauthored a book on the subject called *Less Stress, More Success: A New Approach to Guiding Your Teen Through College Admissions and Beyond*. Written with pediatrician Kenneth Ginsburg, it was released in 2006, one year *before* the scandal broke.

Here is a rare opportunity to look at someone whose professional life has been a web of lies and evaluate what they said at a time when they had no idea those lies would be discovered. Are there any hints in her book about the fraud she was and how she felt about it? And what kind of advice did she dispense to America's youth? I read it cover to cover and found much of interest.

What did Jones have to say, for example, about honesty? How did she feel about exhorting readers to be paragons of virtue even as she was living a lie every day of her life? Urging that students be up front, Jones wrote that, "[telling the truth] is what healthy adults do . . . Do we really want to teach them [the students] that it is okay to lie, cheat, or steal to get ahead in life? Remember that your kids are always watching you."

So true, but who was watching Jones? And why in God's name would she emphasize the very issue on which she was most vulnerable? Was this her way of dealing with the guilt she felt about her actions? After lying for so long, coming clean would have meant admitting that she had been dissembling for decades and that was too hard to do.

Perhaps telling others to be honest was a veiled warning of the conflicts and consequences facing those like her, who lead double lives. Apparently though, she could not bring herself to brazenly lie about her own credentials in the author's bio on the book cover. Either that, or she figured she'd be caught. It's also possible that Jones "compartmentalized" and convinced herself that she was actually two people—one who had the degrees, the proof being her high position at MIT, and one who did not and knew it.

One can surmise that her fabrications must have caused Jones much discomfort, even anguish, and almost constantly. Listen to the following quote from her book: "If you do not live honestly, you will draw suffering into your life because you will always be afraid of being caught." How well she knew that reality! But after rising to the most important job in her career, she could not bear to lose it by telling the truth. It was too late for her, so she did the one thing she could—admonished others not to follow in her path.

Did Jones have a premonition, a belief that a day of reckoning would come for her? Who knows, but the following observation she made was prophetic, to say the least: "Holding integrity is sometimes very hard to do because the temptation may be to cheat or cut corners. But just remember that 'what goes around comes around,' meaning that life has a funny way of giving back what you put out."

And finally, one can see a tone of genuine regret in Jones' literary voice as she discourses on the lengths to which students are willing to go in order to be admitted to that top college, be it MIT or another school: "Is the prize worth any cost?" she asks. "Even denying who you are?". Today, I'm sure she would agree it's not.

A little more than two years later, Jones resurfaced as an education consultant, ready, albeit at a reduced fee, to dispense advice to both parents and admissions offices. There's no question she has what to say and that she possesses valuable contacts, but what about the trust that people need when they put their children into the hands of a dishonest person? The fact that they would and Jones' reappearance proves yet again that scandals in America do not mean it's over. Apologize, wait, and count on the public to forgive, forget, or ignore your past. And also —stonewall. In an interview with the *New York Times* in December 2009, Jones refused to discuss the MIT debacle, declaring simply, "I've put that behind me."

We shouldn't underestimate the high cost of admitting wrongdoing. For South Carolina governor Mark Sanford, owning up to his affair meant the end of his career. No more governors' mansion, no more adulation as a governor; instead he was seen as a hypocrite who sinned even while invoking the importance of religion in his life and presenting himself as a model family man. Everything goes up in smoke, it seems. Facing these consequences, it's no wonder he told his aides to say he was hiking the Appalachian Trail when he was really off the reservation in Argentina with his mistress. But, as usual, lying—the easy way out—is often not the easy way out. The fact is that no one in high office can escape the collateral damage, not Colorado's Gary Hart, not North Carolina's John Edwards, and not Nevada's John Ensign.

FAME AND FORTUNE

There are rumors that Jones was undone because of jealousy about the success of her book. She must have realized the risk she was taking by raising her public profile. For so many people, however, the possibilities of fame and fortune are too appealing to resist. James Frey penned a book, *A Million Little Pieces*, about his recovery from drug addiction. It was a highly praised bestseller until it was disclosed that he had made up and exaggerated much of his account.

Being selected by Oprah Winfrey's book club made it much more likely that he would be found out, but who can resist the possibility of selling a ton of books? The opiate of fame is a major cause of people self-destructing. Like Jones, Frey was forced to publicly recant and apologize, and on Oprah's show no less. Notwithstanding his tainted reputation, he can derive some consolation from the fact that he still sold a lot of copies, about five million. In an unusual move, Random House offered refunds to anyone who had bought the book prior to the disclosure of the lies. There were very few takers.

Politicians are no shrinking violets when it comes to massaging the facts to suit their needs or desires. In the 2005 New York City mayoral campaign, Fernando "Freddie" Ferrer, the Democratic mayoral candidate, posted the following statement on his website: "I was born in the South Bronx and educated in public schools for most of my education. If it weren't for my inspirational teachers and a strong after-school program, I don't know where I'd be." That's nice to know. If only it were true. With a little help from his opponent Michael Bloomberg, it was soon "discovered" that Ferrer attended Catholic schools for all twelve years of his New York City education.

Parochial school supporters were outraged at what appeared to be "parochial self-hatred." But it probably wasn't that. There are far more public school grads in the city than from any other system and Ferrer knows how to count votes. Still, you had to question the man's common sense, or that of the campaign worker who decided to post it. Did he really think he could pull it off? In a debate a month earlier Ferrer may have given a hint of the falsehood to come when he stated that his daughter was a public school graduate when she had actually graduated from Cardinal Spellman High School, Freddie's own alma mater. A Ferrer spokesperson explained, somewhat lamely, that Ferrer "called in some ideas, and someone got a little loose with the editing." Ask yourself how long an error of this magnitude would last on *your* website? It's interesting that it took three weeks to correct it and then only when the opposition gleefully publicized it.

WHEN OPPORTUNITY KNOCKS

Sometimes, to do something crazy or to commit larceny, you have to have the opportunity. And it's the opportunity that causes you to go down the wrong path as you look to get rich, famous, popular, or promoted. Let's say you're there when a truck carrying a lot of cash crashes on a deserted street at night. The money's flying all over the place. You're not a thief, but you're not a saint either. So you take some of it and hope no one notices.

Two months later you try to spend it and get into trouble with the law because the bills were marked. Had you not had a chance to do what you did, you would never have gone out of your way to steal it.

A student borrows her teacher's laptop to download some assignments that she missed. As she's going through the files she comes across the final exam that the teacher forgot to remove. Faster than you can say "cheat," she copies it. Unfortunately, or maybe fortunately, she overreaches and lets too many classmates in on her find and eventually the principal finds out and expels her.

Cheating today has become a high-tech affair (and so have the responses to it). Laser printers reduce crib sheets to a size that can't easily be seen by anyone except the end user, namely the student, and pagers enable youngsters to send answers to each other without attracting more than a minimal amount of attention. In short, there are so many more sophisticated ways to cheat nowadays.

PERCEIVED NECESSITY

Sometimes it's not so much a question of opportunity as it is perceived necessity. A reporter is doing her third story in five days. She's exhausted, but she has a deadline. She can do the story right but she just doesn't feel like it. So she filches five lines from a wire service and is detected by a computer software program designed to catch such people. Asked why she did it, she responds, "I figured, it's just five lines."

In the film, *Resurrecting the Champ*, the reporter, played by Josh Hartnett, writes a story about a down-and-out ex-boxer, portrayed by Samuel L. Jackson, that turns out to be phony. He is urged to come clean by a fellow journalist and his first response is to say to the person who suggested it, "Why should I? Who will know?" adding, somewhat gratuitously, that it "happens all the time in journalism." It's clear in the story that he feels he must do this to achieve the necessary goal of getting ahead in his profession. In the end, however, he is forced to own up to his mistake as more people find out about it. But the initial reaction is revealing—people are often very reluctant to admit errors and see not doing so as far easier. Another version of this situation is perfectly captured in Tom Wolfe's *The Bonfire of the Vanities*, where alcoholic British reporter Peter Fallow fabricates all sorts of things in order to keep his job at a New York City tabloid.

In some cases, it is indeed true that the likelihood of apprehension is slim. You're not bound to get caught cheating on your income taxes, but only if you keep it to a reasonable amount. I would doubt that the police see most people who go through yellow lights turning red. Nor are people who inflate home or auto repairs apt to be discovered. The system is, however, designed to compensate for such petty crime in other ways, like charging more money for traffic tickets or raising insurance costs. So, in the end, is it so smart to do these things? It seems we get caught anyway, just in a different way.

In many of these cases we rationalize our decisions to cheat. We went through the light because we didn't want any jokes made about our habitual lateness. We overstated the damage to our house because "we really need the money." Ditto for tax fraud. When we're caught, we ruefully ask ourselves, "Was it really worth taking the chance?" Those running Toyota surely must have felt a need to minimize the seriousness of their cars' defects out of fear that the company's reputation would be damaged beyond repair and that they would lose billions of dollars. In the end, they had to fess up anyway. Did they still think it was necessary to hide the facts? And was it worth it?

DOES ALMOST COUNT?

The word "almost" is loaded with meaning. "I almost killed him"; "She almost made it"; "They almost won the championship"; "Close, but no cigar." But in many cases people want that cigar, so badly, in fact, that they convince themselves they won it. This is especially true when you're really close. You say, "If I'd made the shot, then I would have tied the school record for most points in a season." Only you didn't and you know it. Or do you?

Yvette Clarke ran for Congress in Brooklyn, New York, in 2006. Along the way, she claimed to have graduated from Oberlin College but didn't because she was two courses short of her BA. Clarke said that she belatedly found the error, but candidates for Congress shouldn't make such blunders. In her statement to the press, Clarke said,

> I spent much of the day in contact with Oberlin College and Medgar Evers College to retrieve my academic records from two decades ago, convinced of my recollection that I had fulfilled the requirements of a bachelor's degree. Contrary to that recollection, I have now discovered that I remain two classes short of the requirements for that degree.

When you "almost" have the credential, it's so tempting to cross the line.

Clarke may actually have fibbed unintentionally. It may be that she knew that it wasn't true when she first began talking about her background many years ago. But as she retold the part about her educational background over and over again, she could well have come to believe it. Psychologists have developed an explanation for this, called cognitive dissonance theory. It states that when things are out of order with your world and make you uncomfortable, you simply rearrange them in your mind. Aware or not, Congresswoman Clarke won that election. She didn't pay a heavy price, but she did suffer the pain of public embarrassment. Had she told the truth all along, it would never have happened. Think also of how easy it would have been for her to actually complete the two courses, though not as easy as saying she did.

FEAR

Lawrence Feld is a prominent attorney whose specialty is tax law. I'd always been curious as to why people simply neglected to pay their taxes. I could understand cutting a corner here and there but simply not paying anything was sure to be discovered and dealt with severely, so why would anyone do it? Feld has both prosecuted and defended such individuals. Prior to entering private practice, he served in New York as Assistant Chief Appellate Attorney for the Criminal Division in the U.S. Attorney's Office, Southern District. He's also a coauthor of a standard work in the field, *Tax Fraud and Evasion*. I asked Lawrence what were the main reasons why people didn't file returns. He replied:

> There are three types, basically, who don't file. Those who are consciously scheming to evade taxes; those, like Wesley Snipes, who claim they don't have to file because they believe the government has no legal right to collect taxes; and those who are simply afraid to submit a return. In the last category you have a lot of people who lost their jobs, went into debt, or got divorced and just didn't have the money.

All these problems required immediate payment or resolution. But with IRS, they figured if no one's asking, they're okay, so they just did nothing. And they rationalized that they'll pay it back when they can. Years go by and they become more frightened because how will they explain it, and the accumulated fines will be huge. And then IRS catches up with them and they're in big trouble. In the end they exercised terrible judgment and confused what they wished would happen with what actually happened.

LYING IS HABIT-FORMING

Habit is the cause of many a miscalculation. Marilee Jones got into the habit of lying. She had to, over twenty-eight years, either verbally or in writing. And after a while it became part of her persona, no doubt. In fact, she probably could no longer excise it from her social and professional narratives whenever the subject turned to her background. A person says, for example, "I grew up in Tulsa, Oklahoma and then went to Wesleyan. When I finished I moved to Boston because I got into Tufts for graduate school." And in such a case, everything's true except the Tufts part, but it's not so easy to get rid of that part, so you don't.

The longer you do it, the harder it is to stop. As reported in the *Sunday New York Times Magazine*, scientific researcher Eric Poehlman committed fraud for many years in the millions of dollars and was actually sentenced to jail time for it. Reflecting on what he did, Poehlman said, "It [the fraudulent acts] created a maladaptive behavior pattern. I was on a treadmill and I couldn't get off."

Scientifically, the processes described by Poehlman and others are part of the way the human mind often works. Researchers have found that people "store" responses and use them in new situations rather than trying to take everything on a case-by-case basis. This is natural, as I learned in my own work on racial and ethnic stereotypes. If we didn't do this, then we'd have to treat everything as though it were occurring for the first time and then we wouldn't be able to function. Thus when Bill Clinton or Jayson Blair, the disgraced former reporter, were challenged, it was easy for them to fall back on rationalizations they'd gotten used to making.

Earlier in our discussion of greed, mention was made of Stephen Ambrose and Doris Kearns Goodwin, historians who plagiarized at the heights of their careers. Perhaps it was because they felt they were running out of new ideas. But how do people like that, prize-winning historians, lose their moral compass? Well, in Ambrose's case, he might not have had one to begin with. Recent findings reveal that Ambrose's pattern of deception began early in his career, well before he achieved fame for best selling books like *Band of Brothers* and *D-Day*. In 1964, Ambrose began his literary career by becoming a biographer of former president Dwight Eisenhower.

In interviews on *C-Span* and *Charlie Rose*, Ambrose went on and on about how the "hundreds and hundreds of hours" he spent with Eisenhower had completely changed his life. Too bad it never happened. A careful review of the record in 2009 by Tim Rives, the deputy director of the Dwight D. Eisenhower Presidential Library and Museum, established that Ambrose met with Eisenhower only three times and spent less than five hours with him. Moreover, he was never asked by Eisenhower to write the president's biography, as he asserted. Was there a kernel of truth to Ambrose's claims? For sure. He did write what was the definitive biography of Eisenhower. But the stories of access and exclusive time spent with the man were products of his fertile imagination. This is an example of lying starting early and turning into a habit over time.

For Connecticut senator Richard Blumenthal, lying about his military service was something he'd been doing for many years. Typical was his comment to a group of veterans and senior citizens at a ceremony held in Norwalk, Connecticut in March 2008: "We have learned something important since the days that I served in Vietnam. And you exemplify it. Whatever we think about the war, whatever we call it—Afghanistan or Iraq—we owe our military men and women unconditional support."

We do, but Blumenthal did not learn the importance of standing behind the troops from his days on the war front because he never served in Vietnam. How could a person think he could avoid being exposed as a liar while on the campaign trail? Your opponents are out to beat you and are therefore very focused on what you say. And this from a smart man who studied at Harvard and was the state's former Attorney General, a job in which he was responsible for finding out the truth.

All of which demonstrates how emotions will often trump reason. When he first told his fib and wasn't called on it, the result encouraged him to try it again. And after doing so a number of times without detection, he was further emboldened. Over time, it became a habit, an automatic statement to be presented whenever he wanted to embellish his biography. That fact that he served in the Marine Reserve gave him a way of rationalizing it. Wasn't he therefore a military man? And didn't the Marines play a critical role in Vietnam?

There's another consideration and that's the sheer pleasure of how people respond to your lies. When a pastor was asked why he blatantly plagiarized in his sermons, he explained, "It's a pattern you get into. You end up using more and more material." What he didn't talk about was the respect and adulation he received when his parishioners complimented him on his sermons.

THE PRESSURE JUST GOT TO ME

Pressure is yet another motive for choosing the easy way out and it comes in many shapes and sizes. When teenagers drink, smoke pot, and engage in promiscuous sex, they usually enjoy it, but they also do it because of peer pressure. Studies have shown that they know the risks of smoking cigarettes and engaging in unprotected sex, but their desire to be socially accepted and to rebel outweighs their concern about possible harm to their well-being.

Research scientists have been found, in many studies, to feel extraordinary pressure to come up with important findings in their work. The labs need money to continue their work, the scientists need grants to earn a living, and the prestige associated with appearing in prominent journals all contribute. It's not for nothing that they say, "publish or perish," and who wants to perish? A *New York Times* article on research described how Chen Jim, a well-regarded Chinese scientist, stole chip designs from a foreign country and then claimed them as his own. People have asked, whether China in particular, in seeking to enhance its national reputation in research, pushes its scientists too hard.

I had a first-year graduate student who plagiarized a small weekly assignment. It wasn't hard to spot. I simply Googled the offending sentences, and presto, there they were. "Why would she do it?" I asked myself. I mean, if you're going to cheat, do it big time, like on a term paper, but not for a piddling weekly hand-in. I called her in and said, "I'm going to ask you one question, Donna, and please understand that your answer is going to matter a great deal." Holding up her critique of the week's readings, I asked, "Is this your work or not?" Her face turned white. Her body language told the story as she slumped down in the chair and wrapped her arms around herself.

"No," she said in a barely audible voice.

"Why did you do it? I mean it was a little assignment."

"Time pressures," was the soft response. By now, she was no longer meeting my gaze, her head lowered, her eyes seemingly somewhere near the top of her sneakers. A tear rolled slowly down her cheek. The air in my office was beginning to feel very stuffy. I felt awkward, but continued anyway:

"I want you to understand something. Plagiarizing isn't like stealing a scarf from a store. When you plagiarize, you're passing someone else's intellectual ideas off as your own. In that sense, it's like stealing someone's very identity. And in the scholarly world, that's a serious breach. If I tell the chairman of the department, that's probably it for you. In college it's more widespread and often less is at stake; but in a PhD program, it's unacceptable and it might well result in expulsion." In truth, we have thrown out a couple of people for just this sort of thing, so I wasn't exaggerating.

Donna looked at me. Fear was written all over her face. She had given up a flourishing career in public relations to come to New York and study in a major, recognized sociology program and now it was all going to go up in smoke.

"I sacrificed so much to come here," she wailed disconsolately. "But I have no excuse other than that I had stuff due. It was really stupid of me." I looked at her and had an intuitive feeling that she was not putting me on, that she was genuinely sorry. And I was moved to give her another chance.

"I'll tell you what," I said. "This is a hard week for students because it's the end of the semester. But I can't just let it slide, so I'm going to test your desire to stay in the program by giving you an assignment that's doable but not that easy, especially because you have to hand it in within ten days. That is if you want to do it." She nodded in assent without saying anything.

"You'll go to a nursing home in Brooklyn and do the life histories of five elderly people. I'll want you to analyze them from a socio-historical standpoint and tell me what their lives were like and why they turned out the way they did. Focus on family, education, jobs, and, most important, their social life. That's it. I'll see you when you're done."

She was emotionally drained from the conversation and as she stood up to leave, I could see she was trembling, with relief, I guess. She hurried out of my office.

Seven days later, after our last class, Donna knocked on my door and when I answered it, she handed me a manila envelope. "Okay, it's here and I hope it's what you wanted," she said before departing quickly. Attached to the paper was a small envelope with a card in it. In small but legible script it read as follows:

> Let me first say how terribly sorry I am about this whole thing. If ever I felt humiliated, this was it. The intense shame I felt as I sat in your office is enough punishment to ensure that nothing like this will happen ever again. It's compounded by the fact that I realize how close I came to losing my dream, one I worked so hard to fulfill. Thank you for giving me another chance, for believing that I could redeem myself.

Happily, Donna did redeem herself. She never got into any trouble again as far as I know and became an outstanding student. I've never told anyone in the department about her and I never will. Sometimes we meet at a party or colloquium and exchange greetings. I sense she's still very uncomfortable about the whole business and I can't say I blame her.

What do we do about people who "take the easy way out?" It's really one of those Malcolm Gladwell-type gut feelings. Something told me that Donna was not cynically playing on my emotions. Moreover, she was a first year graduate student and had probably not yet absorbed the departmental culture about how seriously we take these things. In this instance I saved a career and am hopeful that she's truly learned her lesson.

A lot of petty theft is a result of economic pressure. When people steal food from a supermarket, it's often because they need it just to survive. In some cases, they are eligible for benefits, but pride can get in the way. During hard economic times, theft from department stores goes up. The same is true of the holiday season. But when they're busted for petty or grand larceny, they often ask themselves, "Was it worth it?"

We all know about the thousands of runaway children in America. Their eyes haunt us as they intrude on our consciences. They're on milk containers, in bus stations, and in thousands of flyers. Their faces appear happy, reminiscent of better times, but we realize that they may be anything but happy now.

Pressure can build up over time and when things become unbearable, the easy solution is chosen because you have reached the end of your rope, so to speak, and must have immediate relief. A teenager is living in a home with parents who are constantly fighting. She's often caught in the middle. She is yelled at, even beaten occasionally.

Finally one day she snaps and runs away, heads for Times Square in New York City and is swallowed up by it. Her parents search for her frantically and when they do find her, if they're lucky, they discover that she's living in abject poverty. Maybe she's strung out on dope or turning tricks. They persuade her to return, again if they're lucky, and do their best to make home a happier place. As for the child, she's glad to be back because her life away from home was far worse than anything she'd expected. But she did it because she was angry and desperate. In short, the pressures had become intolerable. Even when people know they're going to a better place, they may resist it.

The great sociologist Erving Goffman noted in his classic work *Asylums* that patients about to be released from mental institutions often become very apprehensive and "mess up or re-enlist to avoid the issue." The patient is basically asking, "Can I make it on the outside?"

Several years ago there was a story about some prisoners up for parole who were working on a highway detail in New Jersey cleaning up the grassy area that constituted the traffic divider. One of them made a break for freedom and was promptly apprehended. At the time, he had only three days left on his sentence. This is more common than most people think. For many prisoners, jail is actually a secure world and they fear the uncertainties freedom may bring. The rhythm of daily life there provides them with a certain comfort level and predictability.

Release can pose significant dilemmas as they come face to face with the need to carve out a new and independent existence. Sure, correctional facilities do make efforts to prepare those in their charge for the challenges on the outside, but for some it's not enough.

Well then, if they can't handle it, maybe the easy way out, namely bolting for freedom, is the wise decision. They'll return to where they're content. Perhaps it's a smart move in an immediate sense but not in the long run, unless we feel that people who are happy in prison should remain there forever, even after they've done their time.

INTOLERANCE FOR UNCERTAINTY

And now we come to yet another really interesting reason for why people look for the easy way out—the lack of tolerance for ambiguity. Various reasons were given to explain why the Bush administration's nomination of Bernard Kerik for Homeland Security Chief went down the drain. Among them was that he wasn't forthright in his responses and that Bush was blind to the candidate's failings because he liked him personally. Another consideration was, as the *New York Times* put it, "a desire by the White House to quickly fill a critical national security job."

But it's not only Bush's people who needed closure. Most of us dislike leaving matters open-ended. We want certainty so that we can relax and move on. In the next two chapters, when we deal with psychological problems that people have, we'll get to the root of this pattern. For now, let's focus on how it works. In a fascinating experiment, economists presented people with the following two choices: One box contained fifty red caps and fifty black caps. The second box had a mix of one hundred red and black caps, but it was not known how many there were of each. People were offered a two-hundred-dollar prize if they picked a red cap. Which box do you select to make your choice from?

Most people decided on the first box, where they knew the exact total number of each color. Social scientists refer to this as "ambiguity aversion." People like certainty even if it doesn't, as was the case here, necessarily increase the odds in their favor. They have little tolerance for ambiguity. Thus, when they experience too much of it, they can be pushed or persuaded into making a bad decision simply to relieve their anxieties.

This is what happened to Dave Birdwell. He went to a Friday night party for company employees. After a few drinks, everyone's tongues loosened and Dave told a joke about a man who stuttered. It was funny and everybody laughed. Later, as he was driving home, he told his wife about the joke and how he felt he had made a good impression with it. Suddenly, he put his hand to his head and exclaimed, "Oh, my God!"

"What's the matter?" his wife asked in an alarmed tone.

"I think John Hexter was there; he's the VP for development. He's got a speech defect too. He lisps. Do you think he might have found my joke offensive?"

"I don't know," his wife responded. Then, trying to reassure him, she continued, "Are you sure he heard it?"

"I just don't know," Dave answered. "But he was standing nearby. I'm just not sure he was listening."

Dave tried to put the incident out of his mind, but he couldn't. After a sleepless night, he determined that he had to do something about it and soon. He resolved to talk to John on Monday. He'd find a way to bring it up casually, without making it look too obvious. He got his chance when he met John in the washroom.

"Great party," he said. "That was a pretty tasteless joke I made the other night about stuttering. I guess that's what happens when you have too much good booze," he finished, with an uneasy laugh.

John looked at him in momentary confusion. "What joke?" he asked. "I didn't hear it." Then, fixing him with a somewhat hostile gaze, he barked, "Anyway, I don't think speech defects are a funny topic," and stalked out.

Dave was mortified. "If only I'd kept my mouth shut," he moaned. The guy hadn't even heard the joke. And now he would think ill of him. All because he had to get it over with. Clearly, it would have been wiser to have waited to see how John related to him. Then, if he felt animosity from him, he could have tried to make amends.

WHY IT'S SO HARD TO COME CLEAN

Life can get pretty complicated at times, yet another reason why people take the easy way out. Whether you're Marilee Jones or Quincy Troupe, the poet laureate of California who claimed a degree he never had, it's hard to admit wrongdoing because it's often such a hassle clearing things up. You have to tell people like employers or close friends that you deceived them in the past. Sometimes that can even include your spouse, who's not necessarily going to be so forgiving. "You could have at least told *me*," she'll say. "I'm you're wife, after all." So, in the end, hiding things may just be easier.

Pragmatic considerations can also be responsible for someone keeping quiet. You've heard the nasty stories about your good friend, about what a jerk she is and how she doesn't care about anybody except herself. But what good would it do to tell her? She'll just get defensive and you like her for many reasons. For one thing, she's been your friend for twenty years, ever since you met in high school. Meanwhile, your friend doesn't realize that because people can't stand her, her husband isn't going to be admitted to the country club he needs to be in to get the business clients he wants. So you've chosen the path of least resistance out of fear she'll "kill the messenger," but you now also bear some of the blame for the fact that her family is going to suffer. In the end, what's "easy" for you, isn't going to be for her.

Nobody likes to lose what they have. In a celebrated case, the huge McDonald's restaurant chain was accused of fooling the public by claims that its French fries were prepared in "pure vegetable oil." Yes, but what it didn't say was that their natural flavor came from beef. Faced with these accusations McDonald's chose the easy way out and countered that they had never claimed their fries were suitable food for vegetarians. When that explanation didn't fly, the restaurant belatedly said they were sorry: "We sincerely apologize for any hardship that these communications have caused among Hindus, vegetarians, and others." They also donated $10 million to various groups as part of a settlement following a class action lawsuit filed against the company.

The longer you have something the harder it is to give it up. People like Marilee Jones who live a lie for twenty-eight years and who benefit from it daily are loathe to throw it away simply for the sake of telling the truth. Coming clean means losing that nice office and the salary and prestige that go with it, plus doing a lot of explaining to colleagues and friends. From her perspective and that of almost anyone else in her shoes, it's just not worth it. And she had by all accounts done a good job. Interestingly, one study of women who feel they're "impostors" in real life, showed they had strong desires to succeed and competed harder. Of course, if you'd told Jones that one day her misdeeds would make the front page of the *New York Times*, that's different, but how could she have known?

Marilee Jones was well-liked and highly respected at MIT. When the news came out, colleagues and students expressed deep regret at her predicament. One freshman, Mike Hurley, summed up the prevailing sentiment when he said, "Whenever someone's integrity is questioned, it sets a bad example, but I feel like the students can get past that and look at what she's done for us as a whole."

However, the esteem in which Jones was held also meant that she did have an option. She could have confided in someone whom she trusted and actually gone to a respected college and earned a degree, over time, appropriate to her position. I know someone in a similar position who did exactly that. It's anyone's guess whether that would have worked here, but it would certainly have been very time-consuming and exhausting at the end of a long day in the office. Which is why I call not doing so, "the easy way out."

Jones had to go through the typical "gatekeeper" to obtain her first position, namely a person who decides whether or not one should be hired. What's interesting is that the position she had, deciding on who does or doesn't get into MIT, was a gatekeeper's job par excellence. In a sense, the very nature of the position may have unconsciously had a particular attraction to her precisely because she was a fraud. Being a gatekeeper may have given her a feeling of safety, however illusory. Illusory, because she wasn't even passing on what she had lied about, people's professional credentials. She was determining who gets into college, a completely different area.

In addition to the material losses a person suffers when they admit to wrongdoing, real psychological damage results from publicly losing face. Exposed frauds can become pariahs, as those who respected or envied them, depending on the case, now see them in a completely different light. Richard Blumenthal and Mark Sanford will always be perceived as liars, no matter what becomes of them. This explains in part why owning up to their tall tales proved so difficult.

Many of the people who lie about their credentials are very talented. In fact, that's why they've been able to get away with it. You're practicing dentistry in a developing country where they don't check up on you like they do in the United States and you're very good. You do excellent crowns and caps and root canals. People come from all over to be treated by you. The fact is, you never finished dental school. But you look at the reputation you've established and the thousands of people you've seen over the last twenty years and it seems preposterous to you, on the rare occasions when it pricks your conscience, that it should matter whether you really have that "stupid piece of paper."

And that's in a field where the knowledge is directly relevant. But what if, like Congresswoman Yvette Clarke, there's no real correlation between having an Oberlin BA and being a successful legislator? You've passed laws that have benefited your district. You've given speeches that have inspired your listeners. You've really done things. So whether or not you actually have the degree seems almost irrelevant, and if it looks good on the resume, why not? The same holds true for Quincy Troupe. You don't have to own up to not having actually graduated from college. You've written thirteen books, including six volumes of poetry and now you're the newly crowned first poet laureate of California. It seems a shame to rain on your own parade by revealing something about your past that has nothing to do with your present. That is, until others find out about it.

OPTIMISM

I know someone whose wife worries a lot. It's her nature. Her husband doesn't. That's his nature. He jokingly says, "I told my wife she's in charge of worrying for the family. Why? Because she's going to worry anyway." The husband acknowledges that he has an overly optimistic personality. "Secretly, I'm glad she worries because I need someone to make sure I don't become unrealistic in my hopes and expectations. She's the realist I need." But he continues to have his dreams. Why? Because that's him.

People like that can sometimes get into trouble. They're the kinds of people who, when told they have to check out the shaking in their car at 65 mph with their mechanic, decide not to because it's easier to ignore it. Then, when they break down on the highway because the ball joints are completely worn down, they're sorry. It's the person who has that third or fourth drink in the restaurant and insists on driving home because "I can handle it." Then, when he's stopped by the police and busted, he says to his wife, "It was really dumb. I should have called Tom and asked him to drive me home. He lives right near us."

We're all different in our personalities. Many people have a feeling of invulnerability. They think it'll never happen to them. And even when it does, they dismiss it as an aberration. They have a belief that things will turn out all right. This leads them to ignore lurking dangers or problems that could have been solved without becoming so complicated. So they opt for an easy or quick fix and sometimes it's just not a good move.

6

INSECURITY

It's something we all have. It's not a clinical term, but we know it when we see it, both in others and in ourselves. It has to do with not feeling confident, comfortable, or even safe. It shows up in many different ways. We may worry about what others think of us—whether or not we're well-thought of, respected, or to put it simply, liked. Some people even need to be feared to be secure.

Outside factors can precipitate or heighten insecurity, like losing a job or failing to get a promotion. A casual remark by others about how we look can set it off, or a joke made at our expense. The refusal, whether passive or active, of someone to do our bidding can make us nervous. The feeling of being ignored or made light of can ignite insecurity and even that higher state of worry, anxiety.

Insecurity by itself is not the kind of thing that makes you go for therapy. But it's something that we live with all the time, every day of our lives. Most important, insecurity can cause us to harm ourselves and others in ways that we can deeply regret. Which is exactly why we need to understand what brings it to the fore, to the point where we can't stand it and end up doing something foolish. It's a complicated phenomenon and has many causes that are rooted in our deepest needs, fears, desires, and hopes.

"I don't care what anybody thinks of me," is one of the most common statements that people make. What they fail to realize is that the very statement shows that they do. They certainly care about what the person they're saying it to thinks or they wouldn't have said it. What they are really expressing is a dislike for *having to care* about what others think. But most of us know this is an absolute necessity for getting through life. It's perhaps best embodied in the famous saying by the former speaker of the House of Representatives, Sam Rayburn: "To get along, you've got to go along."

What causes insecurity? Is it our upbringing? The situation we're in? The folks we hang out with? It turns out to have multiple causes, of which certain basic ones predominate:

1. Concern about social status
2. Control freaks
3. Addicted to approval
4. Feelings of worthlessness
5. Guilt
6. Unwilling to take a chance
7. Feeling useless or helpless

CONCERN ABOUT SOCIAL STATUS

One of the things we care most about is our social status or standing. When we're well-regarded by others, we feel secure. This need is so great that people will sometimes do really foolish things to ensure their status among those who really matter to them. This idea brings to mind an incident that happened about fifteen years ago. It wasn't an earth-shattering event, as these things go, but I remember it well because it brought home to me how sensitive people can be to how others see them.

My wife and I hosted a dinner party for several couples. One of the women present was a tall, slender, and very attractive brunette with a certain quiet charm. She didn't say much, but when she did, you remembered it. She would look at you with a half-smile and you kind of knew that there was more to her than met the eye. I didn't know much about Rita's background other than that she had met her husband, a physician, on a trip they had both taken to Tibet, Nepal, and India. The others around the table were all successful, or success-bound professionals of one sort or another. We were talking about the pros and cons of living in New York, when Rita said something about the advantages of growing up in a small community.

"Where are you from?" I asked.

"Princeton," she responded. Without thinking, I followed up with,

"Did your father or mother teach there?"

"Yes, my father was a professor there," she said, with just a second's hesitation, something I thought about only later.

"Oh, what area?" I asked.

"Sociology."

"Really," I said. "What's his name?" I thought I might have heard of him.

"Charles Bailey," she said. "But he wasn't there that long." The name was unfamiliar to me, but I didn't think about it much, as the conversation soon shifted to other topics. Besides, what with some thirteen thousand active sociologists out there, how can you know everybody, even at a prominent university like Princeton?

A few days later, the phone rang. It was Rita. "I have to talk with you."

"Sure," I replied. "What's on your mind?"

"Well, it's something personal and I'd rather talk to you face to face."

"Okay," I responded, a bit concerned now. We met the next day in a coffee shop in Manhattan, near where she worked. After exchanging some pleasantries, including what a nice time she and her husband had, Rita looked at me solemnly and declared,

"Listen, there's something I have to tell you. It's really crazy. I lied when I told you my father was a professor at Princeton. The truth is he was just a maintenance man there, actually an assistant foreman at the university's physical plant." I was certainly surprised to hear that and responded:

"So why did you say he was a professor?" She looked at me uncomfortably, almost beseechingly, and groaned.

"I didn't know what else to say. Everyone's so status conscious here. I couldn't say he fixed boilers."

"But you didn't have to say professor. You could have said he was in business."

"'Professor' was the first thing I thought of since you're one."

"Did you have to pick sociology, my own field, where I know people?"

"I know, I know," Rita said in an exasperated tone. "That was *really* dumb. But I heard you say that was your subject and so it was the first thing that came to my mind. Anyway, that doesn't matter anymore. I just didn't want you to think I was a liar."

Needless to say, I've changed some significant details in the story to protect her privacy. What's interesting is it shows how much we care and how close to the surface such anxieties are. We're talking about a well-to-do woman who lives in a nice home, dresses beautifully, and drives a nice car. In short, she's "made it" by conventional standards. Yet somehow it's not enough to make her feel relaxed and secure about herself.

Status insecurity is a wider problem in our society. Most people live relatively anonymous lives. They are not interviewed on the radio or television, or written about in newspapers. Their achievements are never noted or commented upon beyond their own circle of friends or perhaps those who reside in their neighborhood or hometown. For some people, this feeling that they don't matter, that they're insignificant in the larger sense, can lead them to do things to get attention. This is especially true of teenagers who may act out by committing acts of vandalism. Graffiti, for example, while it can be a form of art or even protest, is often a way of getting attention by youngsters who feel alienated.

Those who have status are often the object of resentment and this resentment can sometimes emerge in unguarded moments. I was conducting a market research study and I heard a conversation in which a jewelry saleswoman was explaining to a customer how the firm offered buyers of its jewelry a "certificate of authenticity." But in an interesting, and quite possibly telling slip of the tongue, she referred to it as a "certificate of 'ostenticity,'" a made up word that sounded a lot like *ostentatiousness*.

When we are praised our sense of having status is clearly enhanced. The question is, how much praise is enough? That depends on the individual, but problems can arise when people who work or live together have widely differing opinions about it. I know couples whose marriages suffer because one party feels the other doesn't sufficiently appreciate them. "I don't mind taking out the garbage at night when it's cold outside, but you'd think she'd at least thank me for it. But she just takes it for granted. I hate that." In one case, two people working on a volunteer project parted ways because one of them felt their contributions to it were not being recognized. Good managers and leaders know that everyone needs a little massaging and some, more than a little.

Paradoxically, too much praise, especially from the wrong quarters, can lead to dangerous and even reckless acts. Many insecure people surround themselves with sycophants, an entourage of gladhanders who tell them what they want to hear and that they can do no wrong. Sensing that you thrive on being flattered and that failure to do so will bring about their own demise, they fail to warn you of the negative consequences of, say, ignoring the law, or refusing to fulfill the terms of a contract, even when they know that what you're about to do is really stupid. They're afraid that you will "kill the messenger" and ignore the message. Were you a more secure individual they wouldn't have been afraid to tell you what you needed to know to avert disaster.

I'M IN CONTROL—YOU'RE NOT

We've all heard the term *control freak*. While most of us aren't like that, for many folks, control over others, events, or most importantly, their own destiny gives them a feeling of security. Traumatic events can establish this need for control. Kids who saw him as an outsider and "different" bullied Judge Sol Wachtler while he was attending elementary school in Blowing Rock, North Carolina. Though he was resourceful and adaptable, he no doubt felt relatively powerless when one day a group of kids ganged up on him and beat him to a pulp. The reaction as an adult can be a desire to amass enough power to be secure. Rising to the position of Chief Judge of New York State certainly qualifies.

Just about everybody comes late once in a while. Usually it doesn't matter much provided you offer a sincere apology or have a good reason. But sometimes it can hurt you. You arrive late to a job interview. The interviewer forms a bad impression and you're not hired. He thinks, "If he can't show up on time to something important like an interview, what does that say about how he'll do on the job?" You're thirty minutes late for a key business dinner and your fellow diner gets fed up and leaves. The painful result for you is a lost contract.

Many people take someone else's lateness as a personal affront. They may see it as an indication that you think your time is more important than theirs. Indeed, that may be precisely what you do think! Too bad they now know it.

What's really behind it, though? Why is it that some people are always late? Some of the chronic ones may be insecure in general, people resentful of having to seemingly "give in" to others' priorities or needs. In short, they have authority or control issues. Showing up late is their way of rebelling. This can lead to broken relationships, lost friendships, or missed business opportunities, outcomes that people don't want. Often they know deep inside that this is inappropriate behavior and the punishment they frequently receive for it becomes an almost subconscious way in which they verify their own feelings of inadequacy.

On the other hand, many latecomers can simply be absentminded people who have a hard time organizing their lives. The same is true for those who "forget" to pay bills or parking tickets. They may even be perfectionists who have great difficulty concluding or letting go of whatever it was they were doing before their next appointment. Such individuals can clearly not be "blamed" as being deliberately late. Regardless, they can often end up paying a high price for their minor offenses, like a permanently bad credit rating or no electricity in their home. Unfortunately, many people often fail to recognize that such people feel genuinely bad about their forgetfulness or desire for perfection, choosing instead to vilify them.

Another behavior relating to control or authority is borrowing items and neglecting to return them. This can cause difficulties, especially when, as in a favorite baseball bat or brooch, it's something of importance to the lender. The outcome can be a strained or even severed friendship. Again, for some the problem is simply forgetfulness.

If you're an insecure person you may anticipate that you're going to be attacked even when it's not in the cards. A little dose of paranoia often helps grease the wheels in such cases. Say you think someone is saying bad things about you. To prevent what they're saying from being treated credibly by others, you start telling tales about that individual. As it turns out, they haven't been saying anything about you, but now, when they hear what *you're* saying about them, they retaliate in kind and you end up with an enemy who can cause you serious harm.

For many individuals personal space, or territory, is very critical. It is a way of protecting oneself against possible attack. The more secure you are, the less likely you are to feel invaded if someone encroaches upon it. Watch what happens on a bus or subway. Some people become extremely edgy if another person sits too close to them. Others don't seem to mind. Sometimes space is a matter of protocol. Remember the flap that ensued when Michelle Obama touched Queen Elizabeth? In that instance it was a matter of creating social distance in order to protect one's status. Clearly the English view such matters differently than do Americans.

A person asks someone to move their car out of their driveway. Failure to comply leads to violence. Those responding in this manner are doing so because they feel personally threatened and insecure. They see the encroachment as an attack on their own safety and even integrity.

ADDICTED TO APPROVAL

Joseph Ellis, a professor at Mount Holyoke College, regaled his students with stories about his Vietnam War exploits. The problem is that he wasn't a war hero. In fact, he hadn't even been in Vietnam during the war. His "war service" was limited to three years teaching history at West Point, just as Richard Blumenthal's service was confined to a stint in the Reserves. The fact is that exaggerating or fabricating military exploits is not uncommon, perhaps because many insecure people need to demonstrate to others how strong and courageous they are.

It's not as though Ellis was an anonymous scholar in the groves of Academe. He was and is one of the most prominent historians in the United States, winner of the Pulitzer Prize in 2001 and a National Book Award in 1997. Ellis was quite specific in his lies, telling his classes that his duties included working on General William Westmoreland's staff in Saigon, and clearing out enemy positions in infamous My Lai while serving as a paratrooper in the 101st Airborne Division. The students listened spellbound as he spun his tales. What a man, they thought. A real war hero and a brilliant professor.

Had he limited himself to his captive audience, he might have gotten away with it. But, in a self-destructive manner reminiscent of Gary Hart's dares to the media, he repeated these accounts to the *Boston Globe*. What's more, he moved into other areas of his life, telling reporters that he was so disturbed by what he had seen that he joined the peace movement, another lie as it turned out. To top it off, he told the *Globe* that he had scored the winning touchdown in the final game of his high school career. Would that it were true! Alas, he wasn't even on the football team.

Why did he do it? What was the source of his insecurity? Most people exaggerate at times, but this went far beyond that. As a nationally acclaimed scholar, Ellis surely had enough prestige. He didn't need to burnish his credentials. Such blatant lies suggest a strong desire to be caught and punished. In that way he could relieve the guilt he felt over having deceived others, something he couldn't help doing because he also wanted to be idolized.

When confronted about his bizarre behavior, Ellis at first declined to respond. Eventually, though, he did and revealed that his father was an alcoholic. He also characterized his family as dysfunctional. Interestingly, his professional integrity as a scholar was never challenged or in question. Unlike fellow historians Stephen Ambrose and Doris Kearns Goodwin, no one accused him or even suggested that he had ever plagiarized. His work is still seen as first-rate by most historians.

It's almost as though Ellis created this Walter Mitty-type of life that was completely divorced from his scholarly one, inventing a character who exhibited great heroism, courage, and determination, be it in war, protesting war, or on the football field. Tellingly, these traits quite accurately describe the people about whom he wrote books—George Washington, Thomas Jefferson, and others. Who knows? Perhaps his immersion in their lives created a desire on his part to be like them, or to be admired like them.

A sure sign that a person's desire for approval is beyond the normal range is the unnecessary lie. Bragging, exaggerating, and even dissembling in ways obvious and sometimes not so obvious are normal behaviors. Making things up out of whole cloth for no discernible gain isn't. Head-hunting is one of the things I do on the side and I'll never forget the case of Ronald Collier. He was recommended by someone for the position of dean at a private high school in Miami. Collier got the job and did reasonably well. When his contract came up for renewal, I was asked, as an objective outsider, to evaluate his performance.

As part of the process, I reviewed his resume. In doing so, I became intrigued by the titles of several articles he'd listed because they were of a sociological nature. I located the journals on the Internet, but when I tried to search the first article, it didn't come up. The same was true of the second, and the third, and the fourth. In fact, to my astonishment, *none* of the articles he'd listed existed, as far as I could tell.

As an academic, I wasn't shocked by the falsification of his resume. It was the *degree* to which it was false that was unusual. People will "double-dip" on publications, for example, listing an article that is essentially a slightly reworded version of another article with a different title. They might count a letter to the editor of a journal as a publication, or list a book review with a title as an article. They might pretend that a popular talk they gave at a bankers' association meeting was an academic presentation. But I'd never encountered anyone who claimed to have penned nine articles and hadn't done any of them. This guy even had the gall to put "In French" in parentheses for one of his pieces, presumably to impress the reader with his "international" reputation.

I've always operated on the premise that those who lie in one area are apt to have lied in others too, something that turned out to be true of Stephen Ambrose as well. With that in mind, I called up the Ivy League institution from which Collier claimed to have received his doctorate. Well, you guessed it. He didn't have it. Oh, he had gone to the school, but only for one semester. They threw him out for unspecified reasons. I could just imagine what they were. I was not surprised when it turned out that a grant he claimed to have received from the

National Endowment for the Humanities was also limited to the realm of his fertile imagination.

Of all these lies, it was the one about the articles that most perturbed me. I could understand claiming a degree when you didn't have one. That's far from unheard of. The governor of West Virginia's daughter, Heather Bresch, did that, too. And the grant Collier listed was about education. With a degree and a grant, you could ask for more money. It made sense to lie about those. But the articles? High school deans, unlike college professors, aren't required to publish anything. There was nothing to be gained from it.

I met and confronted him with what I had found, or rather, didn't find. At first he denied it, but when he saw I had him dead to rights, he owned up to it. "Why did you do it?" I asked him.

"Because I was depressed," Collier replied. "I'm in therapy. You see, my father was tortured in the Korean War and never got over it. My shrink says I do these things because I didn't live up to the expectations people had of me when I was a child. I was seen as something of a child prodigy. I read very early, I was valedictorian of my elementary school class."

I told the story to a psychiatrist friend of mine and asked her what she made of it. "I can only speculate since I don't know him, but it's definitely a familiar type," she said. "There are many possibilities. He may have felt that he should write brilliant articles that show how he fulfilled the great things that were in store for him. In essence, he couldn't bear not living up to his image, not being as talented as people thought he was. So he created an image that pleased him, one in which he was *Dr.* Collier, author of highly respected articles, and fluent in a foreign language. In this way he could get the approval he so desperately craved. And unless his therapy really helps him, which means that he has to want to change, he'll likely do it again. He can't help it. No matter how much he's praised, it'll never be enough."

She was correct. Years later, long after he'd been forced to resign his position, I spoke with someone from another head-hunting agency who told me that he'd applied there too and the doctorate was still listed. But I guess there had been some progress since at least the articles were no longer on it. I also learned through another source that his father had never served in Korea either. A sad story, it demonstrates just how damaging insecurity can be.

FEELINGS OF WORTHLESSNESS

When people can't stand success, they are prone to self-destruct. That's what happened to Joseph Ellis. It's also what happened to Bill Clinton, and when we reflect on what happened to him we see that the need for approval is only part of the issue. Underlying it are feelings of worthlessness, a belief that you don't deserve your good fortune in life, namely rising to the presidency of the United States. In his autobiography, there is a section in which Clinton discusses the Monica Lewinsky affair, or rather, his affair with Monica, devoting, in total, about ten pages to it, which comes to about 1 percent of the book. It was surely unpleasant for him, but he couldn't avoid it in a work titled *My Life*. In it he writes, "What I had done with Monica Lewinsky was immoral and foolish. I was deeply ashamed of it. . . . "

Nowhere in the book does he directly explain why he did what he did, but the answer is there, albeit indirectly. Clinton was ambivalent about his Army service. He knew that joining ROTC gave him a good shot at avoiding Vietnam, but, as he put it: "somebody will be getting on that bus in ten days and it may be that I should be getting on it too." Most revealing is the following observation:

> My struggles with the draft rekindled my long-standing doubts about whether I was, or could become, a really good person. Apparently, a lot of people who grow up in difficult circumstances subconsciously blame themselves and feel unworthy of a better fate. I think this problem arises from leading parallel lives, an external life that takes its nat-

ural course and an internal life where the secrets are hidden. When I was a child, my outside life was filled with friends and fun, learning and doing. My internal life was filled with uncertainty, anger, and a dread of ever-looming violence. . . . At Georgetown, as the threat of Daddy's violence dissipated, then disappeared, I had been more able to live one coherent life. Now the draft dilemma brought back my internal life with a vengeance. Beneath my new and exciting external life, the old demons of self-doubt and impending destruction reared their ugly heads again.

Clinton's explanation is palatable to him because it blames his circumstances and because it effectively turns him into two separate individuals, one of which is good. The bad individual is the one who played around with Monica. It was self-destructive and Clinton probably realized that he was likely to be caught. But once caught, the punishment and public humiliation could justify the feelings of worthlessness he has described so well in his own words. In a way, the more successful he was, the more he achieved, the greater the disparity between the two selves became. The widening gap must have made it even harder for Clinton to reconcile them.

Dr. Jack Nass is an extremely thoughtful psychiatrist blessed with an ability to think creatively. That's why I turned to him as I pondered Clinton's fall from the good graces of the American public. His soft voice belied an intensity of feeling about Clinton that came through quite clearly as he shared his thoughts with me. It quickly became apparent that he didn't think much of Bill:

Clinton fits into something we psychiatrists call "the self-defeating personality." You won't find the term in the official diagnostic manual but it exists as a type. He had an abusing alcoholic father. There's also an overindulging mother. That's the background of such people. Imagine how Clinton would have felt had he finished his presidency with honor, won the Nobel Prize, and become a world statesman, like Jimmy Carter. And in the back of his mind, he knows he pulled one over on the world. He had attained this great position but he had done it with guile and deception. One part of him would feel wonderful, but the other part wouldn't.

Nass obviously agreed with Clinton's self-assessment of the two parts of his personality. I asked him how this applied to Lewinsky: "He was conflicted about being caught. He felt he'd escape as he'd done many times before. Lewinsky will recant. Why not? He'd paid off women in the past. In truth, by staying on as president, he did get away with it to a degree, even if he did get impeached."

In this astute interpretation, Clinton sounds a lot like the chameleon-like character Zelig created by Woody Allen. His complexity cannot hide the basic insecurity and belief that he's something of a fraud, that he doesn't belong up there with the great leaders of the world. It's a feeling that comes through in his own writing and it's what led him to hurt himself.

GUILT MAKES THE WORLD GO 'ROUND

There's nothing wrong with having some guilt. It's an emotion that prevents us from letting our desires and impulses go wild and we all have it to some degree. The feeling of guilt about having something you don't deserve operates at every level. I have a tennis partner who is ten years younger than me. If I go head-to-head with him, returning his hard shots with my own, I will invariably lose because his hard shots are harder and better than mine. The only way I can beat him is to slow down the game and place my returns out of his reach. Then he's playing my game and I usually win. Occasionally though, I feel as though I don't deserve to win if I hit it softly, that it's not fair, and so I revert to the hard shots and end up losing. That is my punishment.

Sometimes it's not good fortune but bad that makes someone feel guilty or undeserving. In his book about why otherwise honest people shoplift, psychologist Will Cupchik describes a man who shoplifted because he felt guilty about persuading his wife to have an abortion when he was beginning his own career. He felt a baby at that stage in his life would limit his chances for success. Unfortunately, she was unable to conceive when, a few years later, she tried again. The husband just couldn't forgive himself.

Guilt can also come into play when someone does us a favor. A classmate gives a child a toy. Then the friend asks her to slip an answer to her on a test. The child complies, is caught, and gets a zero. A friend asks you to take their daughter to an amusement park. You don't really want to because you have a headache, but you remember that your friend baby-sat for your kids last week. You go and, after standing in various lines for hours with the sun beating down on your head, you get a terrible migraine, a malady to which you're prone. You feel awful and curse yourself for having agreed to go. The last thing you remember thinking before you pass out is the familiar refrain, "No good deed goes unpunished."

Guilt can sneak up on you. Take the case of Dr. Y, who was given a perk by a drug company. At the time he wasn't asked to do anything. Later on, however, he wrote an article about Alzheimer's disease and available treatments for it. His feelings of obligation because of the perk he got caused him to play down some minor side effects of the drug company's medication. He did this not out of greed but because, in the back of his mind, he wanted to repay them for that nice week in Hawaii they had given him. And then people learned of his trip and accused him of having compromised his integrity for a free vacation.

The gift doesn't even have to be large to be effective. In fact, small gifts to physicians are even more effective than large ones. This is because the very size, or lack of size, of the gift makes it seem harmless. And when the person reciprocates he can convincingly say he did it out of conviction. After all, how could a paperweight, a nice pen-and-pencil set, or a free dinner compromise a person of his stature? And yet, given the psychology of gift giving and receiving, they can. That these baubles are effective can be seen from the very fact that pharmaceutical companies give them out. Not surprisingly, a larger gift is more likely to be rejected because it would be seen as an obvious bribe, though, as has been said many a time, everyone has his or her price, or at least almost everyone.

Insecurity, in combination with guilt, can actually cause people to do the wrong things repeatedly. Let's say we feel deep down that something we have done is wrong. But at the same time we want to do it anyway. Doing it over and over enables us to justify it anew each time and each time we get away with it, it serves to convince us that it must, therefore, be all right to do it. Unfortunately for those who would rationalize their misdeeds in this manner, repeated wrongdoing also increases the chances of apprehension.

Say, for instance, you shoplift. You justify it by saying the department store can write it off, everyone does it, you need the item more than they do, it's not a big ticket item, whatever. But you know at some level that it's wrong to take what doesn't belong to you. One way of dealing with the dissonance is to keep doing it. Then, when and if nothing happens to you, it can begin to seem like something that's okay to do.

UNWILLING TO TAKE A CHANCE

Did you ever wonder why people don't try something new even when it's good for them and they know it? When personal computers first became popular, millions of people, mostly middle-aged and older, refused to consider them. "I'm old-fashioned," they said, or, "I like it better the old way," holding on to their IBM Selectric II as if it were a life preserver. Did you ever experience the frustration of trying and failing to get someone to adopt your way of doing something, be it enrolling in a better medical plan or using a Blackberry as a planning calendar?

Sure you did. Happens all the time. The reason, psychologists say, is that most of us are "risk averse." We've gotten used to doing something a certain way and we don't want to change. Sometimes we're right, but usually we're not. There's a reason why most people start doing something differently, namely it's a better way to do it.

When people irrationally resist innovation they are reflecting a certain degree of insecurity, even fear, at the idea of changing. This is much more ingrained in us than we suspect. In one experiment, college students in two classes were asked to answer a questionnaire. Each class was rewarded for participating. One got a decorated mug, the other a large Swiss chocolate bar. Before leaving the class, however, students were given the choice of trading in the gift they'd received in exchange for the other one. But very few did, with 90 percent of the students choosing to keep what they had.

Psychologists have coined the term "status-quo bias," to explain this type of behavior. It's a sort of "the devil you know" attitude. A good example is where you're promoted to a new position with increased responsibilities and you worry whether you're up to the task. But you know if you stay where you are you won't get that raise, that nice window office, that secretary, that longer vacation. So you take the plunge—or you don't.

Writing about the steroids scandal for the *New York Times* Op-Ed page, former Major League baseball player Doug Glanville wrote:

Yes, baseball players are afraid. Not just on opening day and not just because of the 400-page Mitchell report and not just because of a Congressional hearing on performance-enhancing drugs in baseball . . . but because they have always been afraid. A player's career is always a blink in a stare. I retired at the ripe old age of 34 following a season of sunflower seeds and only 162 at-bats. I had been a starter the year before. In this game, change happens fast. Human nature wants to put the brakes on that rate of change.

Implicit in these comments is the idea that change may be for the worse. This often translates into a desire to hold on to the known and the familiar, regardless of whether or not the change might be beneficial.

FEELING USELESS, OR HELPLESS

Glanville raises another issue that breeds insecurity: the fear that we'll become helpless or, in the case of the aging ballplayer, useless. His comments on this topic speak to the heart of why so many players were reluctant to inform on their teammates even if they themselves were innocent. As he writes with heartbreaking honesty, "And, in the quest to conquer these fears we are inspired by those who do whatever it takes to rise above and beat these odds." At the same time, he makes a rare appeal to higher altruistic values when he observes, "We call it 'drive' or 'ambition,' but when doing 'whatever it takes' leads us down the wrong road, it can erode our humanity. The game ends up playing us."

Fear of helplessness is especially prevalent among the sick and the elderly who are, in fact, frequently helpless. Such fears can take over a person's life and seriously impair their judgment. A doctor fails to explain a patient's condition to their satisfaction. He or she may be too busy or insufficiently empathetic, but the result is the same. Fearing the worst, a common enough tendency, the patient falls into a depression. They may even commit suicide in the belief that their death is imminent and likely to be unbearably painful.

Psychiatrist Dr. Philip Levine is a highly sensitive and caring man who works closely with disabled adults. So I thought he'd be able to help me comprehend the impact of feeling abandoned. He surprised me by sharing the following fascinating vignette:

Psychiatrists who want to be analysts must go through analysis themselves as part of their training. One time, Levine went to see his analyst and told him that he was a bit disturbed to see a FOR SALE

sign outside the analyst's house. The analyst didn't respond directly, but told him to check the sign again on his way out. When Levine looked at the sign, he discovered, to his amazement, that it actually read WET PAINT!

"That's incredible," I said. "What could it have meant?"

"A number of possibilities came to my mind," he replied. "The most obvious one is that I feared he was going to leave the area, move away, and I'd be left without my analyst while I was still in the middle of my training. Another thought was that maybe it means I think *he's* for sale, meaning his granting me my license to be an analyst. And maybe WET PAINT meant I'd lose him temporarily and FOR SALE meant he'd be permanently unavailable."

Whatever the correct answer, the emotions associated with the fear of abandonment must run deep if even a trained professional can make errors so loaded with meaning.

The young are equally vulnerable. As children, we were dependent on others for protection. We were insecure about our inability to defend ourselves against anger from others, violence, criticism, or humiliation. When, as adults, we feel threatened in similar ways, we can be reminded of those days. And when we are reminded of them, we may do stupid and risky things that we believe will prevent us from being vulnerable.

I once knew a professor who had grown up in Germany before World War II. Carl and his wife, Joanne, were friends with my wife and me. We'd go to concerts together and have dinner at each other's homes. I didn't know much about his prewar experiences, but I imagined that, as a Jewish kid growing up under the Nazis, he'd gone through quite a bit of suffering before coming to the United States in 1938.

We moved to a different community and I lost touch with them. But then one day, I don't remember what triggered it, I called them just to see how they were doing. Joanne answered the phone:

"Oh, hi. How are you doing? I haven't heard from you in ages."

"I know," I said, apologetically. "I should have called sooner. Anyway, what's happening with you and Carl these days?"

"You didn't hear?" she said. "You don't know?"

"Know? Know what?" I answered, concern rising in my voice.

"Carl's dead. He died three years ago. He killed himself."

"What!" I was stunned. He'd always seemed like the most level-headed guy in the world, hard-working and dedicated to his research, but not a workaholic. He had a wry sense of humor and seemed upbeat and completely devoted to his wife and children. "How could this happen?" I asked.

"Well," she said almost matter-of-factly, "here's the story in brief. Carl was the chairman of the physics department here. He'd been chair for a long time, nine years, but they liked him, he was good at it, and they kept reelecting him. Then, there were some faculty members who thought a younger person should do it. So they elected someone else. You're probably thinking, big deal, but for Carl it was a catastrophe."

"Why?" I asked.

"Because the election took him back to his childhood. Carl was raised in a small town in Bavaria, one with very few Jews. One day, the Nazis took over the local government and they told the townspeople that Jews could no longer attend the local public school. Carl had no idea what was coming. He went to school in the morning like he always did. When he walked in, the teacher grabbed him by the ears and physically threw him out the door. He was shocked beyond belief, especially when he heard the kids laughing at him and calling him 'dirty Jew.' He was eight years old at the time. He went home and told his parents. They were horrified, but there was nothing they could do. Not long afterwards, they left for America.

"Carl never forgot it. 'My whole world vanished in an instant,' he'd say to me whenever we spoke about it, which was quite often. The election brought it all back to him in a very painful and debilitating way. He felt he'd been rejected by his colleagues. He sank into a depression and never came out of it. We tried to get help, but he was resistant. One day, I came home and found him lying in bed. He'd overdosed on his pills and he was gone."

The story was deeply distressing to my wife and me. Even now, as I write these words, decades later, it's still very upsetting. An exceptional case, no doubt, but it's the unusual that so often illuminates the normal, for stories like this represent the outer margins of the fear and insecurities we all have. Cases like this help us grasp the emotions that churn beneath the surface and which rise up when our sense of safety and security is violated.

7

ON THE EDGE

I t's hard to say what's "normal" and what's not because the word *normal* is such a general term. Still, most people would agree that there is a range of behavior between the normal and the psychotic. For example, if you're upset about getting a speeding ticket, your first in ten years, that's normal. If you lose sleep for days over it, you're what I'd call, "on the edge." If you mourn your recently deceased sister for a period of time, that's normal. But, if two years later, you still can't get on with your life, then there's a problem. If you're angry with someone and decide not to remain friends with them, that's normal. But if you start calling them up at 2:00 a.m. and breathe heavily into the phone, you're *really* on the edge, but you're probably not psychotic or, if you will, "over the edge."

If a problem interferes with your normal functioning or behavior, it means something else, possibly serious, is going on. Even within that category, there's a broad range. A person can be taking medication, like Valium, because they feel anxious. But when he or she takes it more often than prescribed, or in combination with other drugs, it can become a case of substance abuse. There are clinical terms for some of the more serious forms of being on the edge—depression, paranoia, obsessive-compulsive disorder—but even there, people with these illnesses can vary in how seriously affected they are. They can and often do continue to live relatively normal lives, working without disruption at their jobs, going to the movies with friends, and the like.

Nevertheless, the phobias, anxieties, and illnesses from which they suffer can sometimes cause them to act irrationally and they can well end up doing things that are seen as crazy, self-destructive, or just plain stupid. That's why it's very useful to try to get a handle on the underlying causes for such behavior. We're not talking about conditions in which people are divorced from reality, like paranoid schizophrenia, but rather the garden-variety problems that allow people to go on with their lives while, unfortunately, impairing their ability to do so.

WHAT DRIVES US TO "THE EDGE"?

We're all different in terms of what and how much we can tolerate. We all have pet peeves and things that can frustrate us. And a variety of circumstances can cause us to explode. As we'll see, plumbing the depths of human behavior is a highly complex challenge. But there are, nevertheless, some general causes of "on the edge" behavior that apply to most people. I have divided them into the following broad categories:

1. Clinical psychological issues
2. Substance abuse
3. General stress
4. Thrill seeking

CLINICAL PSYCHOLOGICAL ISSUES

When Emotions Run Wild

When we think of astronauts, we think of people who are the epitome of stability. We see their confident, fresh-looking faces in the newspaper or on TV and we just know we can trust them. After all, they represent the best that America has to offer, patriotic individuals who are both highly motivated and very disciplined. We also know about the careful weeding-out process they have undergone to be selected for their appointed task. In short, they're an elite group of citizen heroes.

That's why Americans were astonished to learn about the strange case of Captain Lisa Marie Nowak, an astronaut whose career disintegrated before our very eyes. On February 5, 2007, seven months after her first space mission, Nowak was arrested in Orlando, Florida at 4:00 a.m. and charged with the attempted murder of a fellow astronaut. That was weird enough, but it was the bizarre details that riveted millions to the news accounts about her.

Furious over the romantic relationship between Captain Colleen Shipman and Commander William Oefelein, Captain Nowak decided to do something about it. Nowak (who was married) and Oefelein had a two-year affair that Oefelein was trying to end. She drove 950 miles, without stopping to rest, from Houston, Texas to Orlando to confront Shipman. Her planning for that encounter sounded like something you'd see in an action film. She disguised her appearance, wearing a black wig over her blonde hair. In her car, police found a steel mallet, a knife, pepper spray, four feet of rubber tubing, latex gloves, garbage bags, and a compressed air pistol. Not wanting to be delayed in any way from her mission, Nowak reportedly wore a diaper, thereby eliminating the need to stop anywhere except to fill up for gas.

According to the police report, Nowak said that the pistol "was going to be used to entice Ms. Shipman to talk with her." Apparently, so was the pepper spray because Shipman was attacked with it when Nowak, wearing a trench coat, met up with her in an airport parking lot. When it happened, Captain Nowak had gone without sleep for over twenty-four hours. Looking disheveled and disoriented, she was released on bail and returned to Houston after being fitted with an electronic device that could monitor her comings and goings. To no one's surprise, NASA dismissed her a month later, even while expressing sympathy for her personal predicament. She continued to be employed by the Navy as a curriculum developer for flight training.

Lisa Nowak became the subject of late night TV jokes and her escapades even formed the basis for a *Law & Order* episode. She was portrayed as a wacko by a rapper named Common, who proclaimed in the song "Drivin' Wild": "Doing all that she can for a man and a baby/ Driving herself crazy like the astronaut lady." A parody, one could say, but regardless, it contains more than a grain of truth. Be it love, thirst for revenge or power, or a desire for fame, it is in such instances that the rawest of emotions bubble over and cause people to commit mayhem. Lisa Nowak's journey is a prime example of it.

Her background provides tantalizing clues to her aberrant behavior. She became fascinated with space travel when she was only six years old. Motivated by a burning desire to succeed, Nowak logged some fifteen hundred hours of flight time. She went through a grueling training program to become an astronaut and doing it as a woman was even harder. It's fair to say that people like her do not accept failure at *anything* with equanimity.

Yet no one at NASA picked up any signals that she was careening toward disaster. And maybe it wouldn't have happened were it not for one development—Nowak and her husband had separated just weeks before Nowak went into "space rage." But that is often the case when people lose it emotionally. There's a precipitating event that drives them over the edge, especially when combined with whatever efforts she was making by phone and in person to win back her lover. Add to that a long trip that allows an already furious person to become angrier and angrier with each passing mile and you have an explosive mix.

Love denied, in particular, has the capacity to infuriate people almost beyond belief, perhaps because the desire to possess *someone* is much greater than the wish to possess *something*. We convince ourselves that we just cannot live without the other person and what can be more powerful than that? Just look at the case of Lisa's fellow Texan, Clara Harris, who ran over her adulterous husband, killing him. And what about the Belgian moll who watched delightedly as the woman she suspected of having an affair with her boyfriend fell thirteen thousand feet to her death? She had rendered her supposed rival's parachute inoperable. The woman, Els Clootemans, reportedly tampered with Els Van Doran's cords. She was charged with murder and attempted to commit suicide prior to questioning by the police.

Many have argued that the source for such behavior also lies in the physiological makeup of the human brain. When I asked Dr. Herman Davidovicz, a neuropsychologist, about this, he noted that, "The left prefrontal lobe of the brain controls emotions while the right lobes are where those feelings are expressed. If the left lobe doesn't work right, that makes it easier to become frustrated and do something rash." I asked Davidovicz whether this meant that we couldn't control our hardwiring. His answer was enlightening: "Some of it is due to hardwiring and some of it has to do with the environment. But what you have to remember is that hardwiring isn't necessarily permanent. It often changes in response to environmental factors."

Bipolar Disorder

Bipolar disorder, or manic-depressive illness, if not properly controlled with medication, can lead to pretty disturbing reactions, some of which can cause grievous harm to either the sufferer or those around him or her. Basically, it's a disorder characterized by extreme mood swings from euphoria to depression that become uncontrollable. The manic state is especially dangerous. Dr. Jack Nass, a psychiatrist specializing in this area, gave me an example from his files:

"I had a patient who, in a manic state, decided that he could drive his car head-on into an eighteen-wheeler truck and survive. That's pretty self-destructive, right? But he didn't think he was going to die. To *him,* it's not self-destructive to do that. At that moment your judgment is so bad you think you can survive it. It's very different from, shall we say, Bill Clinton, who knows he can be destroyed."

"Did the man survive it?" I asked.

"Yes he did. I guess he was right," Nass said, with a chuckle. "Seriously though, I think he hit the truck at a low speed and not directly. He did end up in the hospital. I told him, 'Don't try it again. Don't push it.' On medication, he wouldn't have tried it."

"What happened to people who were bipolar before there was medication for it?" I asked.

"They became prophets; they became Jesus or Abraham. In reality, it was the manic depressives who were often our leaders in the old days."

Nass compared the manic state to "having amphetamines pumped into your system from within. You're euphoric and there's no turning it off. In fact, it gets more severe as it goes on and becomes a truly painful state to be in."

Britney Spears, who has sold over 70 million albums, has engaged in some rather off-the-wall behavior. In addition to the pressures of fame, a messy divorce, and child-custody battles, clinical explanations for her antics ranged from multiple personality disorder to postpartum depression to bipolar disorder. Certainly there were plenty of signs supporting the manic thesis—virtually nonstop clubbing, making a public display of shaving her head, looking like a wild woman as she was being carried out of her house strapped to a gurney, whacking a car with an umbrella—the list goes on and on.

In January 2008 I interviewed the former chief justice of New York State's Supreme Court, Sol Wachtler. Why? I was curious to learn what happened to him and how, fifteen years later, he felt about everything. He still lives in Long Island. It is home to him. Dressed in a gray sweater and neatly pressed tan pants, Wachtler greeted me warmly. I looked into his eyes and could immediately see that there was still plenty of charm and life in them, dulled only slightly by the passage of time. At seventy-seven, he was still vigorous and alert.

The former chief judge has not stood still. He's written a successful crime novel, called *Blood Brother*, and he lectures regularly, mostly about the criminal justice system. Wachtler recently regained his law license and teaches a course at Touro Law School. Clearly, he has been rehabilitated, yet he bears the scars of his ordeal. "I know today I'll never be able to live it down," he says almost pensively. "But thank God, I have family and friends, including the judges I worked with, who have stood by me through the years." He has a passion—changing the way mentally ill prisoners are treated. Wachtler knows first-hand because of what happened to him:

"Just like with me, when mentally ill prisoners act out, they're placed in solitary confinement and that makes matters worse. So I've worked to help introduce legislation that would change that. I'm convinced that we'll succeed soon. But my main objective is to insure that the mentally disabled are kept out of prison altogether. We also need to raise public awareness of what can cause mental illness. For example, there was some mental illness in my own family. But because of the stigma, I was never told about it and didn't know it when I was arrested."

Judge Wachtler's main defense for his erratic behavior was bipolar disorder, but he acknowledged that it was no excuse for his criminal deeds. As a judge, he should know. Sanity means knowing right from wrong and understanding the consequences of one's actions. Wachtler admitted he was sane and said his illness couldn't be grounds for dismissal of his case. It could, however, and did, in his view, explain his behavior. He argued, therefore, that he should be regarded as someone who was ill and in urgent need of treatment, not as a common criminal.

In situations like that of Britney Spears, where the individual is really out of control, there is no issue of feigning mental illness for any gain. But in Wachtler's case, the possibility is there. What if Wachtler knowingly planned in advance to use a mental-illness argument in case he was apprehended? He would simply say something like, "Consider who I am—a chief judge, a possible gubernatorial candidate, a person who has led an exemplary life. Wouldn't I have to be literally out of my mind to have done this? So it must be true that I was." And that's only if he got caught. If not, there was always the possibility that his manipulative behavior of creating someone who was after Joy Silverman and presenting himself as the one who would save her, might actually result in his getting her to return to him.

It's unlikely, as some have asserted, that Wachtler secretly planned to use the mental illness defense in advance. Why? Because the downside, if he were found out, was simply too great. It meant the end of his career and public humiliation, and the real chance of going to jail, all of which happened. Moreover, being able to claim that he was ill was not exactly a great way to get out of it, especially when we consider that he came from a generation that saw mental illness as something to be hidden.

Then there are those who point to the fact that he had never claimed to have bipolar disorder in the past nor exhibited strong signs of it. True, perhaps, but disease can strike at any time. As to those who say that people who are manic don't generally go to such extremes, that argument doesn't hold water either because we know that people can have widely varying reactions to mental incapacitation. We're all different in that sense.

Obsessive Behavior

Another malady that can be a stimulus for destructive acts is obsessive behavior, wherein a person has unwanted and unmanageable obsessions. If they are severe, they are often classified as obsessive-compulsive disorder. The obsessions, which can sometimes be quite violent and frightening, are generally what get the person into trouble with others. Often the appearance of such symptoms is a warning of bigger problems to come, but people frequently miss those signs.

For example, telephone records revealed that Lisa Nowak phoned her ex-lover, William Oefelein, at least a dozen times and sent him seven text messages, *all in one day*. That's obsessive behavior. The same is true for Judge Stephen Thompson, a former New Jersey Superior Court judge arrested in 2003 for possessing child pornography and for traveling abroad to have sex with a minor. The obsessive nature of the man was apparent from the fact that police found him in possession of fifty-seven computer disks containing literally thousands of kiddie porn images.

Jeffrey Toobin, who wrote a bestselling book about the Monica Lewinsky affair, described Bill Clinton as guilt ridden and obsessed with sex in a compulsive way, given his long history of sexual conquests. Tiger Woods was also obsessed with sex and apparently proud of it. "I will wear you out. . . . When was the last time you got laid?" he allegedly boasted to mistress Jaimee Grubbs on September 27, 2009, according to Us Weekly. In fact, it would be fair to characterize it as an addiction. To deal with the problem, Woods entered a program in Hattiesburg, Mississippi at the Pine Grove rehab center, called "Gentle Path." It specialized in treating sexual addiction.

Obsessions are by no means limited to romance or sordid topics, but they can be equally damaging. How about the strange obsession of Francis Vitale Jr. of the Englehard Corporation? Apparently fascinated by the concept of time itself, Vitale loved antique clocks and embezzled a whopping $12 million from the company to finance his world-class collection. Now that's an expensive habit! His lawyer said that Vitale was "obsessed to the point that it interfered with his judgment." After the fraud was discovered, Vitale went into therapy, an excellent idea, considering the circumstances. Former Miss America Bess Myerson had already evidenced compulsive behavior in 1980, long before her legal problems and shoplifting escapades occurred. At that time, a police report noted that she sent "dozens" of threatening letters to people with whom she was personally involved.

Obsessive behavior can be directed against many people or, as with Sol Wachtler, it can focus on one subject, in his case Joy Silverman. Perhaps nothing was nuttier than the story of Burt Pugach, a one-time prominent Bronx attorney, who hired three men to throw lye in his girlfriend Linda Riss' face and blind her so that she wouldn't be attracted to anyone else. He was sent to jail for this horrific, obsessive crime. But even crazier, *she married him when he was let out*. This amazing story is chronicled in the documentary film *Crazy Love*.

Like with Nowak and Myerson, there were early danger signals. When his girlfriend broke up with him, Pugach called her repeatedly and even hired someone to throw a rock through her window. And then, prophetically, he told her in a phone conversation, "If I can't have you, no one else will have you. And when I get through with you, no one else will want you." Pugach, as we know, made good on his threat. His story demonstrates the tremendous damage that the mentally ill, diagnosed and undiagnosed, can inflict on their unfortunate victims.

Why did Linda marry him? Because of her belief in "Christian forgiveness," a fortune-teller's advice, a belief that someone else would marry him, and a feeling that the police were somehow responsible for what he did. Mrs. Pugach apparently has a droll sense of humor. When people comment on how beautiful her skin looks, she responds, "Lye is good for the skin but bad for the vision." And her husband displays the same whimsical nature. Asked if his wife holds a grudge against him, he quips darkly, "She doesn't throw it in my face."

These abnormal individuals are of interest here because it is they who do the supposedly "dumb things" we read about. But lesser obsessions are pretty common, too—stamp collectors, women "in love" with Johnny Depp or Brad Pitt, Yankee or Angel baseball fans. There may be a good deal of masochism, but probably obsessiveness, too among people who regularly, almost compulsively, follow terrible pro sports teams like the basketball doormats of recent years—the New York Nets, Miami Heat (at least until LeBron James joined them!), and Minnesota Timberwolves. Even Nass, who treats obsessive-compulsive disorder, has obsessive thoughts occasionally. He told me, for example, with a twinkle in his eye, about what he calls "library dreams":

You're dreaming that you take a book off your shelf and you find it's a library book. You look at the due date and see that it was due ten years ago. Anxious, you run over to the library to return it because you're afraid something terrible will happen to you if you don't. Then, when you get there, you discover that the library is closed for the weekend.

I used to have these sorts of dreams after medical school. In the dream, I'd learn that there was going to be an exam in an hour and I hadn't even known there was a course like this, much less an exam. I'd get some notes from someone and frantically start reading them, but there was no way I was going to be ready in time. I'd run down to the school hoping to get a postponement for the exam and then find out that no one knew where the exam was being given.

Many people have anxiety-provoking dreams, often on the same topic. They regularly have nightmares about missing a bus or a train, or about being in public with no clothes on, about wild animals or giant insects chasing them. But these are within the normal range, an expression of our suppressed fears, probably nothing more.

"Normal" and "True" Paranoia

When a person has an abnormal fear or anxiety about a perceived threat, it's generally referred to as paranoia. We're not talking about paranoid schizophrenia, a psychosis wherein the individual loses touch with reality, hearing voices coming from the sky or thinking there are cameras in the ceiling of their apartment. What is meant here is an otherwise normal fellow who has an exaggerated concern about how others perceive him. When someone says to their friend, "Frank, you're being paranoid," it means "You're worrying too much. Joe doesn't hate you. He's not thinking all day about how he's going to hurt you. No, you've got it all wrong."

Usually in such cases, Frank doesn't have it *all* wrong. He probably has some basis for thinking what he does. That's how the quip, "Even paranoids have enemies," came into common usage. It's just that he may be reading too much into Joe's comments or actions. And it is this tendency, which some people have more than others, that can cause individuals to do things that they later regret or feel stupid about.

In reality, paranoia is best measured by its location on a continuum. The examples of Joe and Frank and those about to be discussed fall well within the normal range. They cannot be considered as mental illness, but they can lead to foolish behavior. Yet they are discussed here because they are similar in kind to paranoid behavior, which is often diagnosed as a neurosis, or worse.

Picture the following scenario: A couple I am friends with was invited to a cousin's wedding and instead of sitting at a family table, was seated with some people who were only invited because they were neighbors and the cousin making the wedding felt obligated to do so.

"Why weren't we seated with other family members?" they wondered. And since they had given, as they found out later by comparing notes with others, a perhaps too inexpensive engagement gift, they concluded that the parents of the bride (their side of the family) were "punishing them" by not seating them with the rest of the family. They were feeling really hostile about it for weeks and had already decided to have as little as possible to do with their cousins from now on. Then, one day, they got a call from their cousins, thanking them for their generous wedding gift. My friends were polite but not very friendly in the conversation. Then, just as they were about to get off the phone, the parents of the newlyweds said, "By the way, we wanted to thank you both for being so nice to our neighbors. They had such a good time at the table with you. I didn't know who to put them with, but I thought you'd be perfect since you're so warm and friendly all the time. Thanks again." End of story.

One of my departmental colleagues was discussing with me the community in which she lived. Her view was that if you invited someone who moved in on your block over to your home for dinner they should invite you back. I asked her why it should be an obligation and she answered, "I don't have to invite people to my house in the first place just because they moved in. But if I go to the trouble of cooking a meal for them and entertaining, then they should reciprocate."

"Okay, I can see the argument," I said. "Is that what other people do where you live?"

"Yes," Annette said, "but, to be honest, I remember one case where I got angry and then I felt like such a dope." Curious, I asked her what happened.

"Well, I invited some people who'd just moved in down the street. They came and had a nice time, or, at least *I* thought so. They were at least twenty years older than us and Steve and I didn't have a lot in common with them, but I still felt the evening went reasonably well. But almost a whole year went by and they didn't invite us back. And I got annoyed. I also thought that since they were a lot richer than we are they probably looked down on us. Steve didn't agree. But he never thinks about these things. 'You're just being paranoid,' he said.

"Well, it turned out he was right this time. Because one day I met the husband in the supermarket and he said to me: 'I'm really sorry we haven't had you over yet, but my wife has phlebitis and she's been in bed and running around to doctors and all. But she's finally on the mend and we'll invite you real soon.' You can just imagine how sheepish I felt."

Annette may have felt "sheepish" as she put it. But she's unlikely to change her approach to things of this sort, nor her views. This is because this kind of heightened sensitivity to slights, imagined or real, is a part of some people's basic personalities. And when people who think this way find that the facts are different in a particular instance, they tend to view it as an exception and return to their ingrained way of thinking after some time has elapsed. It usually takes a cataclysmic event to bring about a paradigm shift in a person's attitude about such matters. Notice how Annette, in referring to her husband, observed, "Well, it turned out he was right *this time.*"

Situations like these should not be confused with slights that are probably judgment calls as to whether or not the person is being paranoid. I remember a rather humorous event that happened to us, humorous largely because of my wife's very sharp response to it. We had invited people in our community to our son's wedding. A year later, the people made a wedding for their daughter. We expressed surprise to mutual friends that they hadn't invited us, though we acknowledged that with weddings there are two families involved and maybe they had a stricter limit on the number of invitees than we had. Anyway, if it wasn't true, it at least gave us the possibility of believing that we hadn't been socially rejected.

Unbeknownst to us, the couple in whom we confided became good Samaritans and took matters into their own hands. They mentioned the conversation to the couple that was making the wedding and they, in turn, decided to act. Now the straightforward thing to do, at least in my opinion, was for them to call and say, "We're very sorry and I know it's late but we neglected to invite you and I hope you can still come because we'd love to have you."

But they didn't do that. Instead, the woman met my wife at a local supermarket and said, "How come we never got your response card?" thereby putting the onus on us. But my wife is nobody's fool. In fact, she's pretty quick on the draw and her immediate retort was, "Oh, really, but we sent it." The woman was speechless because, of course, she knew she had never sent us an invitation. Before she could regain her composure, my wife added, "And we're really looking forward to the wedding."

Exchanges of this sort reveal how much is really going on in the social world in which humans exist and how complicated things can sometimes get. Those whose social antennae allow them to navigate better than others do so naturally. Those lacking such skills commit faux pas left and right and either get hurt, hurt others, or both.

Events like those described above can exact a heavy emotional toll on the participants but they don't have a widespread impact. When they occur among leaders of countries, however, the reverberations can be enormous. We need look at no less an event than Watergate to understand this. When people think of Watergate, words like "third-rate burglary," "scandal," and "political skullduggery," are likely to come to mind.

On June 17, 1972, five men hired by the White House were caught red-handed trying to burglarize Democratic Party headquarters. Their capture helped bring to light earlier instances of burglaries and illegal wiretapping. What really turned the scandal into a major catastrophe for the Republicans that led directly to then-president Richard Nixon's resignation was the attempt to cover up the subsequent investigation. The president himself was directly linked to these efforts and many of his aides and advisers were forced to step down in disgrace, with a number of them going to jail.

Nixon was seen as paranoid and obsessed with spying on people whom he believed were trying to harm him. One could fairly describe his thoughts and behavior as neurotic. While, like all leaders, he had enemies, his efforts to thwart them were seen as over the top. This image had crystallized early in his career when, after a pretty dirty campaign in which he successfully ran for the U.S. Senate in California, he was given the nickname, "Tricky Dick." The name stuck and Watergate was seen as all too typical of his ethical conduct throughout his political career.

Paranoiacs are extremely distrustful and easily offended. They are rigid and incapable of compromise. If there was ever a paranoid leader it was Saddam Hussein. He committed acts of genocide against his own people, started wars of aggression, and was ruthless and deceitful to all, including his own children. In 1995 he persuaded his daughters, who had defected to Jordan, to return to Iraq by promising full pardons to their families. That didn't stop him, however, from murdering their husbands in cold blood three days after they came back.

One might ask why Saddam didn't let the United States or the United Nations into Iraq if, as is virtually taken for granted today, he didn't have weapons of mass destruction. Doing so might well have prevented the U.S. invasion of his country. His failure to extend that offer ultimately caused tens of thousands of deaths, including his own, and graphically portrays how much can go wrong when bad decisions are made by people with power. To comprehend such folly, we need to fully appreciate how flawed the man was.

Jerrold Post, author of *Leaders and Their Followers in a Dangerous World*, sheds much light on this question and provides some remarkable, little-known details of Saddam's relationship with Jews in his native land. Saddam's father died of illness, probably cancer, while his mother was pregnant and his brother died of cancer as well while his mother was in her eighth month. She then tried to kill herself but, ironically, a Jewish family saved her. Then she attempted to abort her pregnancy with Saddam, but again, the Jewish family intervened and prevented it from happening. We can only conjecture how the course of recent history might have been altered had Saddam not been born.

His mother apparently became depressed after giving birth to Saddam and rejected him. He was only reunited with her at the age of three. His stepfather then abused him, both physically and psychologically, rendering him incapable of truly empathizing with others. Some people become depressed and despairing when this happens, but others, like Saddam, react by vowing never to submit to those who would attack them. His violence and viciousness can therefore be viewed as a direct consequence of the traumas of his childhood. And his seemingly irrational acts can be understood as stemming from an almost primal need to respond with lethal force to anyone whom he perceives as an enemy.

On January 22, 2008, a story appeared on the front page of the *New York Times* titled, "In Matters Big and Small, Crossing Giuliani Had Price." In it, the former New York mayor and presidential aspirant Rudy Giuliani was depicted as a ruthless and vengeful leader who would stop at nothing to hit back at those who bucked him. Victims included a chauffeur who complained about a "red-light sting operation in the Bronx," AIDS activists, and former mayors David Dinkins and Ed Koch, whose official photos were removed from the Blue Room at City Hall after they criticized him.

The Times is no friend of Giuliani's, but the accounts of intimidation were, nevertheless, real and true. As one lawyer interviewed for the piece recalled, "The culture of retaliation was really quite remarkable." It often didn't take much to be defined as an enemy either. He was even reported to have borne a grudge against a Manhattan College opponent who defeated him in a class election. Was all this clinical paranoia? It's hard to say for certain and professionals might well disagree on the question. But one can certainly make an argument that it was.

Yet Giuliani could also take credit for tremendous accomplishments. This same individual held the city together after 9/11 in its greatest hour of need, exerting charismatic and powerful leadership and steadying a city whose nerves had been shattered. Moreover, under his administration, crime went way down, the sometimes-excessive influence of special interest groups was reduced, and the city's economy was revived.

There is frequently a duality to people with outsized egos. In defending their harsh reactions to outside threats, they would probably be the first to agree with the oft repeated, "You can't make omelets without breaking eggs." The personality that is characterized by a single-minded obsession with enemies, both real and imagined, is many times also responsible for the focus and positive energy that is so often required to see projects and programs through to completion and to develop an overarching vision that can propel a city forward to greatness. Thinking about New York governor Eliot Spitzer, General Douglas MacArthur, and many other leaders highlights the difficulty, it appears, of having one without the other.

The Lid is Off the Id

"The lid is off the id," might be the best way to describe the deviant type of personality we're going to look at now. In their classic work, *The Psychopath*, William and Joan McCord describe such individuals.

Actually, today the more common term is *sociopath*. He's an aggressive, highly impulsive person who craves pleasure and power and who feels little if any guilt about his actions.

For example, a sociopath bumps into someone on a train. "What do you think you're doing?" the other person says to him. "Go to hell!," is the response. The first person, twice his size, beats the sociopath to a pulp. Why did the sociopath respond so imprudently? Because he lacks the ordinary barriers of anxiety, caution, and most tellingly, a sense that he might have done something wrong.

This pattern of a lack of concern starts early in life. The lesson is: watch out for that kid who pulls the legs off grasshoppers or starts a fire for the hell of it. The causes of such a syndrome? We don't know at this point. It may be due to extreme emotional deprivation or brain damage. The late William "Bud" McCord, who brought me to City College and was a close friend for many years, once told me, "I've seen hundreds of psychopaths and it's one of the most mystifying pathologies around. There's really no known cure for it. The only time you can modify their behavior is if you intervene in the early years of their lives. And even then, the chances for success are very slim." And the damage they inflict can be huge, both as career criminals, and as people who are free and who lie to friends and co-workers, cheat you in business, recommend and perform unnecessary operations, and do loads of other reprehensible things.

We have no better contemporary and famous case of such an individual than Bernie Madoff. From both his actions and his comments he seems to fit the bill perfectly. Madoff cheated people who were very close to him—his sister, people who had been his friends since childhood, and those who had been his biggest and closest supporters throughout his financial career. Even as his financial empire was imploding, he suckered his foremost mentor, Carl Shapiro, into ponying up $250 million, a huge sum that he knew he could not repay. But his victims also included the less fortunately endowed; one said that after losing all her money she was reduced to foraging for food in dumpsters. He made no attempt to warn anyone of impending financial doom and he expressed no regret at what he'd done other than a brief pro forma apology to the judge at his sentencing. Given his history it sounded totally unconvincing. No wonder he received a 150-year sentence.

Psychopaths are characteristically self-absorbed individuals with an attitude of entitlement. Perhaps that's why they are, as McCord noted, people who are very concerned about their physical appearance. Madoff fit into this category too. Though he does not mention it as a trait of sociopaths, Andrew Kirtzman points out in his biography of Madoff that the man "developed a keen interest in his appearance. He adopted a business tycoon's power look, his hair combed back from his receding hairline into a long impeccably groomed gray mane." And who can forget the bemused, smirking half-smile on his face when he was filmed leaving his apartment while out on bail or returning from a court appearance, almost as if it were a deliberately constructed expression of unconcern or even contempt?

Yet another indication of Madoff's sociopathic nature comes, perhaps, from comments he made when he began serving his jail sentence. According to a *New York Magazine* article, he explained that he cheated people who were rich and greedy. As if *he* wasn't. Asked how he felt about those whom he'd fleeced, Madoff shot back, "Fuck my victims. I carried them for twenty years, and now I'm doing 150 years." In his distorted world, there is no justice.

"People in Glass Houses . . . "

When people are guilt-ridden about their lives, they can do some really destructive things. Former congressman Robert Bauman, who represented a conservative district in eastern Maryland, was a vociferous opponent of homosexuality. A married father of four, Bauman made national headlines in 1980 when he was caught having sex with a male prostitute. It was not an isolated incident. As his career came to an abrupt end, he offered up the following mea culpa for public consumption in his book: "Each time I would feel great guilt and head for Saturday confession at St. Peter's or St. Joseph's on Capitol Hill. . . . I would also vow to myself and to God I would never do it again."

Bauman traced his problems back to a twelve-year-old neighbor who seduced him when he was only five years old. The conflicts and self-hatred raged within him as he tried to exorcise what he saw as his demons: "I made up my mind that I was not 'queer.' I heard all these denunciations of homos by my military school peers and firmly resolved I could never be considered one of such a despicable breed."

The pressures of leading a double life can become unbearable and when that happens, people almost welcome being caught, despite the consequences. At a certain level, Bauman was probably relieved that he no longer had to hide his homosexuality. A good indication that this is happening is when the person's acts become more and more brazen.

An argument can certainly be made that this was the case with the disgraced Eliot Spitzer. Going to prostitutes was clearly at variance with his straight-laced upbringing and with his role as a prosecutor of prostitutes. It's called reaction formation syndrome. He had to be aware that such behavior was hypocritical. The signs that he wanted to end it were there. If not, why use as an alias, the name of George Fox, a man who was a good friend of Spitzer's and a major contributor? Why meet the hooker at a well-known hotel like The Mayflower? And why use cash transfers as a method of payment? He surely knew that, given the amounts, they had to be reported to the IRS. These were the very types of transfers that Spitzer had found when he prosecuted others back when he was attorney general.

Ask Spitzer if he wanted to get caught and he will almost surely deny it. But that's because such wishes often operate at the subconscious, or barely conscious, level. And there's no contradiction between this and the earlier discussion of his behavior. A person can engage in stupid acts for more than one reason. In Spitzer's case, the guilt he felt turned him into a crusader, but it was also accompanied by an equally powerful need to dominate others.

"The Unconscious Never Lies"

The "unconscious," as Sigmund Freud conceived it, also plays a pivotal role in the emotional cauldron. In his book, *The Psychopathology of Everyday Life*, Freud famously said, "The unconscious never lies." It's that part of the brain that represents what we wish to do, but have been raised to feel guilty about. This includes anxieties, repressed thoughts, sexual desires, you name it. But sometimes we can't control it. And when this causes us to act out of character, like Lisa Nowak did, we try to explain or rationalize the behavior. What has really taken place, most likely, is that our so-called unconscious has taken over and caused us to act. We cannot explain the acts of the unconscious because, by definition, we aren't conscious of them.

Irene Wineman Marcus is a psychoanalyst from England with impeccable credentials. An author of children's books about bedtime fears and separation, she was one of the last students of Anna Freud, Sigmund's brilliant daughter. I queried her about how this works. After all, Lisa Nowak was quite conscious of what she was doing. Charming, with a quick mind, Irene gave me a disarming smile as she responded:

"Yes, it might appear that way, but it isn't. You see, it's the *motivation* that's unconscious, not the act itself. The act, we're aware of. Let me tell you about someone I've treated. He's a person who still wants to impress his father to gain his approval. And so, even when he's fifty years old, he's still telling his father of his successes. He's not aware that he's trying to show his father that he's more successful than him. In his unconscious, he still hates his father for not having praised him enough as a child, for always holding back."

Shoplifting is one of the most common crimes around. Millions of people do it every year. It's often a crime of opportunity committed on the spur of the moment by people with a bit of larceny in their hearts looking for a cheap thrill, who saw their chance and seized it. There are also those, particularly around Christmastime, who are poor and want what they can't afford badly enough to take a risk. The response is generally a scolding, a fine, or a misdemeanor charge resulting in community service. But sometimes, the causes are much more complex. When that's the case, people don't, as a rule, try to find out what's behind it.

Someone, however, is out there who has seriously studied such instances. The research on shoplifting conducted by the psychologist Will Cupchik is fascinating in terms of how emotions work in indirect ways. Cupchik and his colleagues in Canada have evaluated hundreds of shoplifters and concluded that it's often due to stress, anger, loss, and a desire to manipulate or to avenge something. Typically, the shoplifter steals something inconsequential and can easily afford to have paid for the item. The act of shoplifting becomes a way to fill the void even though, ultimately, it doesn't. Here are some cases that depict how it operates:

A prominent lawyer worth about $2 million was arrested for stealing a tube of toothpaste from a pharmacy. The manager recognized him from a newspaper photo extolling his achievements. He claimed to have no idea why he had done it. Not coincidentally, his four-year-old son had been scheduled for chemotherapy on the very day of the theft.

Bill was a married forty-three-year-old senior vice president involved in a passionate affair with someone in his company. His wife, Dorothy, had no inkling of what was going on. Sally had been pestering him for two years to divorce Dorothy. Bill promised he would, but kept putting it off. Finally, fed up, Sally left him and her job and moved to another city. He got the bad news a few days before his twenty-fourth wedding anniversary. He didn't much feel like celebrating, but knew he had to. So he went to a nearby store to buy a card and some wrapping paper for a gift. Only he didn't pay for them. A security guard spotted him and asked him to empty his pockets. Out came the wrapping paper, the anniversary card, a roll of decorative ribbon and, of all things, a typewriter ribbon. Interestingly, Bill didn't even own a typewriter, so that was really unnecessary. The total value of what he stole was under thirty dollars.

When he called his lawyer, the man's first response was, "Are you bullshitting me, Bill? Do you realize what this could mean to your security clearance rating and to your job?" When Bill had therapy, he quickly came to understand why he'd done it. He was simply expressing his resentment at not being able to extricate himself from his unhappy marriage. Stealing items meant to commemorate the event, and being caught and punished for doing so, was probably a perfect way to express the conflict and guilt he felt about the whole thing.

There was probably a good dose of guilt present in the case of Bess Myerson. When caught shoplifting in a Pennsylvania department store she was under indictment for fraud and conspiracy. The items she had stolen were of little value: a couple of bottles of nail polish, several cheap earrings, a pair of inexpensive shoes, and some flashlight batteries. Ironically, Myerson had once been New York City's Consumer Affairs Commissioner. That's the agency that investigates stores who cheat customers! Psychologists could certainly have a field day with the symbolism of someone like that stealing from a store.

And Myerson was no youngster. It's estimated that half of America's shoplifters are under the age of twenty-five. Myerson was sixty-three when she was arrested. More telling than anything, perhaps, was her reason for being in Pennsylvania at the time. She was visiting Carl Capusso, her companion and fellow defendant in the fraud charges she was facing. How far she had gone from the days when she was respected and celebrated must surely have been preying on her mind, and seeing Capusso could well have triggered her seemingly impulsive act.

Then we have the poignant story of Martha, a nanny with little formal education, who was nabbed by a security guard in a shopping mall after she was observed stuffing two dresses into a large shopping bag. In her home, the police made an astounding discovery. Hanging in a walk in-closet were over *150 dresses, unworn, all with the tags still on them!* What was going on here?

Martha didn't have a clue as to why she stole all these dresses. She clearly had no intention of wearing or selling them or she would have done so. Neighbors depicted her and her taxi-driver husband as quiet, hard-working people, regular church-goers who did quite a bit of volunteer work in the community. Martha told the police, though, about one very curious habit she had. She often sat in the closet, among the dresses, for hours. It made her feel comfortable, she said.

"Why was that?" wondered Dr. Cupchik, who took her on as a patient. After several sessions, Martha revealed that her dog, Yodel, had died around the time she went on her stealing spree. Losing a pet is often traumatic, but it was especially hard for Martha because she was kind of responsible for the animal's death. She'd been preparing dinner in the kitchen when some boiling hot cooking oil spilled on the dog. They were forced to put it out of its misery. Added to all this was the fact that Yodel had been a child-substitute for the childless couple.

But still, Cupchik asked himself, why steal dresses? Why not dog collars or biscuits? And why so many dresses? The answer came as the therapy continued and it was quite shocking. Yet it made absolute sense. Martha had grown up in Europe during World War II. Her father went off to fight. Then, one day, a soldier in a blood-spattered uniform staggered toward her in a field where she was working. It was her father, and as she ran to greet him, he fell forward and literally died in her arms.

And here's where it gets really interesting: Martha's mom, a seamstress, had been ill for some time when this tragedy occurred and they had almost no savings left. In better times, the mother had created beautiful dresses for the wealthy ladies of the town in which she lived as well as for her own daughter. Now these dresses became their ticket to survival. She forced Martha to give up the dresses. She was sent into town to sell the dresses for a fraction of their value or to barter them in exchange for food. And that's how they made it through the war.

Dresses had, as a result, become synonymous with survival. And it had all begun when her father collapsed in front of her. And now, her dog's death had brought it all back, forty years later. The unnatural way in which the dog had died and the symbolic similarity of the liquid oil with the blood on her father's uniform made the comparison even more vivid. It created in her a need to make up for the loss that she was suffering and that reminded her so much of the far greater loss that she had suppressed for so long. What better way to do so than to steal dresses which, in her world, had once been responsible for saving her life? Moreover, these dresses now replaced the ones she had once been compelled to sell and which she had valued.

I have a lot of engineering, computer, and science majors in my large intro-sociology class at City College. In the beginning of the semester, I usually try to explain to them one of the key distinctions between the physical and social sciences: "In chemistry, if you mix solution A with solution B, under the right conditions, you'll always end up with compound C. Why? Because it's an exact science. The same with math. 2 + 2 is always 4. But the social sciences are different. You can know someone for twenty-five years and still not be able to predict precisely what they're going to say next. For me, that's what makes human behavior so interesting. But if you don't like the uncertainty of it, if you have to know *the* answer, this may not be the field for you."

That's what came to mind when I read these shoplifting tales. Human beings are endlessly and amazingly complex. And the connections social scientists make in order to comprehend the mystery of their behavior must often be creative, "out of the box." They can never know for sure if they're right. Often it's a case of it sounding right, like the "aha" feeling you get when something just hangs together. You know it intuitively even if you can't prove it conclusively. That's what makes it so much fun, at least for many of my colleagues and me.

SUBSTANCE ABUSE

We don't need to dwell on it too long, because it's obvious: a lot of the silly, crazy, and ultimately destructive behavior that goes on in this world can be traced to substance abuse. Mel Gibson's anti-Semitic tirade to the Jewish police officer who arrested him might not have happened if he hadn't been drunk. Jayson Blair, whose work included stints at the *New Republic* and the *New York Times*, lost his job amid plagiarism charges and entered rehab, citing drugs and alcohol as major contributors to his problems. Countless others, famous and not famous, rich and poor, have also gone into rehab programs. Diagnosing and treating substance abusers is a billion-dollar-a-year industry.

There is a tendency to equate substance abuse with failure, but it's not necessarily true. A January 26, 2008, headline in the *New York Times* proclaimed, "Death of Troubled Connecticut Surgeon Leads to Charge Against an Employee." The surgeon's career had been wrecked, apparently, by his addiction to drugs. The opening paragraph read

> Ian M. Rubins appeared to have it all. He was a skilled plastic surgeon who treated breast cancer patients in need of reconstructive surgery, and his surgical talents helped him achieve a pampered life, with a $2 million house here [in tony Greenwich, Connecticut], a ski house on 10 acres in Vermont, a 39-foot boat, and a plane.

"So why would he do it?" we ask ourselves, perplexed. But it's never that simple.

Dr. Paul Marcus is a leading psychoanalyst and therapist who treats people with all sorts of problems. One of his specialties is custody disputes. As a forensic psychologist working with the New York State court system, he's seen it all and tells me that substance abuse is a major factor in a multitude of pathologies ranging from family fights to murder for hire. I ask him what causes people to abuse drugs and alcohol.

Marcus is a highly engaging fellow who is not only a practitioner but an intellectual. He's written ten books and maybe sixty articles.

With a full head of wavy hair and penetrating blue eyes, accompanied by a tendency to suddenly burst into joyous laughter when he thinks something is funny or even off point, Marcus gives me a look and fairly hoots at me: "Is that *all* you want to know? Why people abuse drugs and booze? Have you got a month or so to listen?" I tell him to give me the main points as he sees them:

> Okay, here it is. Aside from genetic predispositions, which must also be taken into account, depression and anxiety are probably the leading causes. Plus, substance abusers have low self-esteem and are notoriously impulsive. They can't delay gratification. Drug counselors often fail to understand this. They think it all boils down to self-control—just say no. But if you don't treat the underlying causes, just the symptoms, you never solve the problem. One of my patients jumped a subway turnstile, was caught, and then tried to bribe an officer, offering $500, for which he's now in real trouble. He has a history of cocaine abuse and he said he wasn't thinking. Well, drugs do impair judgment, but his need to take them is deeply rooted in his past. He was abused as a child and has an agitated depression.

Our culture, which promotes the idea that drinking is part of the fabric of social life, also contributes big time. "I need a drink," someone says, and we all nod sympathetically. "Drinks anyone?" your host says at a party. And today we even have scientific research that tells us moderate consumption of wine, preferably red, is actually good for you. The problem is when you drink too much, or take drugs to excess. Needless to say, parental and cultural attitudes, peer pressure, the media, and availability are all part of the picture.

STRESS AND PAIN

Another main culprit is stress. When people are "stressed out" they can easily act out of character. Whether or not they will do so depends on the circumstances and how well they tolerate stress. Often it's a combination of factors that triggers the behavior. Bill and Hillary Clinton entered a counseling program after the Lewinsky scandal. The insight he reports having gained from it applies to just about everybody. In his words, he "also came to understand that when I was exhausted, angry, or feeling isolated and alone, I was more vulnerable to making selfish and self-destructive personal mistakes about which I would later be ashamed."

Leaders in general are more likely to suffer from this syndrome because they're exposed to greater pressures than us ordinary folks. They have crazy schedules, must do with very little sleep, and go through many crises, which is, of course, why they get paid "the big bucks." Still, even if we assume that they're better equipped than others to handle stress or they wouldn't be there, the pressures can become almost impossible to bear. Look at how Jimmy Carter seemed to age during the Iranian hostage crisis. And what about Richard Nixon's heavy-handed response to Watergate? John F. Kennedy also made some major errors when he let his advisers persuade him to invade Cuba in 1961.

In March 2006, Claude Allen, President George W. Bush's former domestic policy adviser, was charged with stealing several thousands of dollars' worth of merchandise from department stores, including Target and Hecht's. The scam involved getting refunds for items he never bought. It turns out that Allen was a pretty straight-laced kind of guy, a nondrinking evangelical African-American and a Republican who professed to believe in the party's emphasis on individual responsibility.

On the surface, his behavior seemed inexplicable, not only because of the deed itself, but because he appeared so successful, meeting regularly with the president in the White House, where he had his office. But beneath the surface, there may have been problems. He had been disappointed at not being named to a federal judgeship, and he had a brother who had some run-ins with the law.

But most of all, he may have felt the stress of being a black Republican. Allen's mentors included the ultraconservative Senator Jesse

Helms and Supreme Court Justice Clarence Thomas. He had been severely criticized by fellow blacks for opposing the Martin Luther King
Jr. holiday. On the other hand, his position at the White House was
one where he had almost no power. The pressure of being viewed as a
"token," of feeling he had to lead an exemplary life as a representative
of his people, may simply have gotten to him.

Sometimes it takes only one event to create the stress that precipi-
tates an irrational response. One psychologist had a patient, a seventy-
five-year-old family man who, after having a few drinks, donned a
Halloween mask and robbed a local 7-Eleven. According to the police,
the man, a first-time offender, was a very polite robber. What set him
off? He committed his crime shortly after hearing that his wife had
been diagnosed with terminal cancer.

The precipitous fall of actor Michael Richards is a perfect example
of how much damage stress can do to someone's life. Richards became famous as the screwball character on *Seinfeld* known as Cosmo
Kramer. When the show ended, everyone had to move on and do
something else with their lives. Richards eventually went into stand-
up comedy, but he wasn't especially good at it and one night he was
heckled by some black audience members during a performance at the
Laugh Factory in West Hollywood. Suddenly, without warning, Richards exploded. And it was not just who he was and the fact that his
comments were racist that left an indelible mark in the public mind. It
was the vivid imagery he expressed, which, unfortunately for him, was
recorded by an audience member and wound up on YouTube: "Fifty
years ago we'd have you upside down with a fucking fork up your ass!
You can talk, you can talk, you're brave now, motherfucker. Throw his
ass out. He's a nigger. He's a nigger. . . . " And that was only the beginning. The stream of invective went on for a full three minutes. And
then it was over, and so was Richards' career.

But there's more to it than simply stress, being unable to control
oneself and lashing out. Sure, the man's career as a comedian was not
going well and this was stressing him out. His previous huge success

on *Seinfeld* must have made the contrast with his flagging fortunes even greater. But the choice of words also reveals deep anger, tremendous hostility, and deep-seated cultural prejudice. In this area, Richards was so clueless that, in a transparently desperate effort to save his professional life, he told Reverend Jesse Jackson "some of my best friends are African-Americans." It seems we've heard that before.

The fact that people weren't laughing at his jokes didn't create his views, it only brought them to the surface. And his rage was only a symptom of his problems. Underneath it all were strong feelings of insecurity about who he was. It's one of the root causes of bigotry. Anger-management training is a good place to start and Richards did get some counseling for it, but it's only a beginning.

On a personal note, I'm a big fan of *Seinfeld*. Now, when I watch the old episodes and see Kramer, I find it hard sometimes to avoid thinking about the things he said, and to just relax and enjoy the show. It's why I've always tried to not know the political and social views of movie stars. Years ago, there was a slogan that flashed across the screen in theaters: "Escape. Go out to a movie." The less we know about who these master role-players are in their real lives, the easier it is to escape from reality and have a good time.

Most of the time, shoplifters are run-of-the-mill people no one has ever heard of. But once in a while someone like the actress Winona Ryder bursts onto the scene. When arrested in 2001 for stealing items from a Saks Fifth Avenue store in Beverly Hills, she attracted worldwide attention. While people often bemoan the light sentences given to the famous and influential, it can also go the other way, depending on pressures to "do the right thing" and on the judge's inclination. Ryder didn't get off so easy. She had to do 480 hours of community service and pay restitution to the store plus a fine and her career apparently suffered, as well. Except for a costarring role in *Mr. Deeds* in 2002, we haven't seen much of her since.

Was there some reason why a star who had received two Oscar nominations and a Golden Globe Award would walk out with stuff she could easily pay for? In an interview several years later, Ryder revealed that as a result of breaking her arm two months before the shoplifting incident, she'd been put on strong painkillers and had continued taking them after she no longer needed them. In fact, charges were made during her trial that she'd been taking medications without a valid prescription. Was this just an excuse? Impossible to know for sure, but since she had no past history of such behavior, the painkillers, which can result in confusion when abused, could well have been the reason.

Physical pain or illness can be an important factor in people's out-of-character behavior. When you're sick and feeling lousy, you're not in your normal frame of mind. You anger more easily, you take offense more quickly, and you're much more apt to see everything in bleaker terms. This is so widely accepted that people don't hesitate to use it as an excuse. "I'm sorry about what I said, but I'd just been told by the doctor that I needed an operation," or "I'd been feeling miserable for weeks about my back, so when she said that to me, I just lost it and belted her." When it's a minor reaction, we understand, but what about when it's not?

THRILL SEEKING

Several years ago, my wife came home one day and said to me, "You know that intersection where there's a camera set up to take a photo if you run the light?"

"Yes," I said. "What about it?"

"Well, I ran it and I think the camera light flashed, so I probably got a seventy-five-dollar ticket."

"Really," I said, genuinely surprised. "You must have miscalculated."

"Actually not quite," she replied. "To tell you the truth, I could have stopped in plenty of time, but I just decided to gun it and go for it."

My wife hadn't gotten a ticket for a moving violation since 1976, thirty-two years ago, when she was charged with going twelve miles over the speed limit and she still disputes *that one*, arguing that their radar must have been faulty. I mean, she's a super cautious driver. That's her only ticket ever.

"That's not like you at all. So tell me, why did you go for it?"

She looked at me for a moment and then, with an enigmatic smile, quietly said, "I don't know why. The devil made me do it, I guess."

That answer stuck in my mind. Why do people do these out of character things? I mused. Was there really more to it than a spur-of-the-moment decision? By the way, she still can't explain it to me.

I asked Dr. Steven Luel, a psychologist, about it. His answer was:

> You can't know what's going on for sure. But she could have said— and the decision was probably made in the blink of an eye—"I've been good my whole life. I never really do anything wrong. To hell with it." I know I've done such things myself, on occasion. I've sat here in my office and it's time to put twenty-five cents in the meter, but I'm in the middle of writing something and I don't want to be interrupted. Or I'm on a phone call that I don't feel like ending, though I could. And then it costs me thirty-five dollars and I feel stupid. But I know why I did it. I gave in to the emotional need of the moment, which was to be cozy and comfortable.

Luel's explanation of my wife's behavior sounded right. But what my wife did was a bit different than what he did with the meter. First, in his case, he was busy doing something. My wife was just cruising along, with no pressure to get anywhere fast. Second, and this goes to the heart of the matter, there was a certain thrill in getting away with it. The reason that Steve mentioned, "I've been good my whole life," might be why many people do things that seem to have no gain.

This idea of having been a responsible person and then wanting to break out, is sometimes called a "mid-life crisis." It has become almost a caricature through frequent use. Thus, if a husband buys a convertible or a wife starts wearing tight fitting clothing at an age when she shouldn't, "mid-life crisis" is the first comment made by others. But there's a measure of truth to it and the reason is that nobody wants to get old; no one wants to feel that their powers are declining. And so we do what we can to slow things down, to pretend it's not happening. And that can lead to rash decisions that one can come to regret, including fights that leave lasting bitterness, irresponsible acts, or affairs that end disastrously.

Many of us just have a desire to do something we don't ordinarily do and also, to get away with it. Certain settings appear to have almost been designed to permit it. Take the annual office party, for example. A vice president at a company portrayed it in the following terms:

> I'm a pretty conservative guy. When we have our Christmas party, people often see it as an excuse to act out and have fun in an acceptable context. So at our party last year, some of my employees were pushing me to drink in the name of fun. "It's a party," they said. I went along with it and had a few because I know everybody needs to break out once in a while. And then later they said, "It was a great party. We got Dwight drunk."

Here's an example, though, where the risk for harm is far greater: I spoke with a law student at an Ivy League school who went to a bar with some of his friends. While there, they got into an altercation, which featured a shoving match that they lost. He and his friends went home, continued drinking until they were really tanked, and decided to return to the bar for a second confrontation. They drove back at 90 mph and were really drunk. Yet they got there too late. The other group was gone.

Only later did it occur to the guy how they had risked their entire careers and even lives with this reckless act. What if they had been stopped and arrested? What if their car had crashed? It begged for an explanation. His answer: "My life is such a cookie-cutter model. It's boring. You want to step out once in a while. It was a thrill to do it."

There is evidence that young people are increasingly experiencing such crises. In their book on the subject, *Quarterlife Crisis: The Unique Challenges of Life in Your Twenties*, Alexandra Robbins and Abby Wilner point out that more and more young adults are acting out because their lives and their futures seem to be so uncertain. And in a *New York Times* interview, a twenty-seven-year-old Yale graduate talks about how he married his high school sweetheart and became a super-salesman at a major corporation. "But I didn't feel fulfilled," he lamented. "That started the snowball." He divorced his wife, quit his unfulfilling job, and returned to his hometown in Pennsylvania.

Boredom is definitely a component, sometimes in combination with wanting to prove something to yourself and others. Teenagers love to go on roller coasters. They call it "fun." The "fun" is the adrenaline surge they get. As Paul Marcus puts it, "Adolescents have an over-stimulated nervous system. They like to ride a motorcycle, say, at 100 mph. That's the age when the shift takes place." And, they may well take secret pride when someone else says, "Oh, I'd be scared to do that." They feel powerful, omnipotent, and have a need for mastery.

As adults, these urges tend to dissipate, but not for everybody and not entirely. The rhythms of daily life are often accompanied by a search for "mini-thrills," though we don't identify them as such. A key manifestation is waiting until the last minute to do something. You create anxiety, almost to give yourself the pleasure of relieving it. Racing to catch a bus or writing a report at two o'clock in the morning that you could have begun much earlier are good illustrations of this.

Not everyone derives so much pleasure from this. For some, it's downright nerve-wracking. I know a businessman who always arrives early for an appointment. He claims not to like the pressure of being late, the anxiety of having to make explanations or excuses. He also has another reason, which may or may not be a rationalization:

"When I show up early," he observes wryly, "it gives me the edge in the meeting. They feel guilty if they show up late and I've got them on the defensive, which, in a business meeting, is exactly where I want them."

Those with excessive yearnings for adventure have an option. They can channel them into professions that sanction or even reward them. That's what spies are like and they're good at it. But it's not for everyone. There are people for whom danger is not only unpleasant, but something they wish to avoid at all costs. They're the kind of person whose palms begin to sweat profusely when an airport security officer asks them to empty out their pockets even though they have nothing in them that would bother anyone. These people are clearly not suited for a career in espionage and they usually know it.

In his essay, *The Imp of the Perverse*, Edgar Allan Poe wrote:

> The impulse increases to a wish
> The wish to a desire
> The desire to an uncontrollable longing
> There is no passion in nature so demoniacally impatient
> As that of him who, shuddering upon the edge of a precipice,
> Thus meditates a plunge.

In the June 2009 issue of the respected journal, *Science*, Daniel Wegner, a Harvard psychologist, reports on research that shows that having such impulses is perfectly normal and that a vast majority of people have them, though they rarely enact them. Wegner's studies shed light on the motives of those who do. He found that to avoid telling your boss that he's a jerk, you have to first imagine doing exactly that. The problem is that when you act it out in your brain, it thus becomes more real and you may end up doing it anyway.

Wegner says that stress may play a role in determining whether or not one "goes over the edge." But taking chances may even have a genetic aspect with other recent research pointing in that direction. Scientists have found that those regarded as "daredevils" may actually be lacking a certain gene, called NeuroD2. This absence is associated with an almost total lack of fear and can therefore cause risky behavior.

Whatever the reasons for "on the edge" behavior, the good news is that, like other problems, it can be controlled and even prevented. What it requires is a recognition that professional help may be necessary. And in cases that do not rise to this level, a combination of exercises and absorbing insights about what causes such behavior may be enough to do the trick. These and other solutions are the subject of the next and final chapter.

8

MAKING THE RIGHT DECISIONS

Bad decisions are everywhere. They are made countless times a day all over the world. People mess up their relationships by fighting, arguing, ignoring, and, above all, not reading each other correctly. In the business world, decisions backfire constantly; from banks that allow employees to sabotage their systems, as happened in France, to huge mistakes in gauging the viability of the mortgage market. Ever wonder about all those stores with "For Rent" signs? Many of them represent someone's failure. They thought their restaurant would succeed. It didn't. They thought their boutique would make it. It didn't. A training program for secretaries was established. It failed.

This book has dealt with the emotional reasons why people make mistakes, why they do dumb things. The first step toward correcting a mistake is admitting you made one. The second is to understand why you made it. And the third, to which we now turn, is finding a way to avoid making the mistake again.

The forty-two ideas, approaches, and suggestions presented here are offered with the proverbial grain of salt. I advise reading them slowly and carefully because, out of a desire for clarity, they may sound deceptively simple. Some are very hard to adhere to because they require a lot of resources, hard work, and a commitment by forces larger than us. Others are easier, provided we have the motivation to try. In all cases, understand that talk therapy, cognitive therapy, and medication should be used whenever necessary. However, developing insight and understanding, along with willing yourself to follow some simple rules or suggestions, can go a long way. That's what this chapter is about. Needless to say, these steps can be supplemented by reading the hundreds of self-help books that provide detailed approaches with all sorts of guidance and mantras.

WE'RE ALL IN IT TOGETHER: HONOR THE SOCIAL CONTRACT

1. In a diverse country like ours, people from different cultures are constantly thrown together. In light of that, efforts have to be made to force people to meet and get to know each other. Most of the time, people work with each other in a 9-to-5 situation but don't meet in relaxing circumstances other than at the annual Christmas party. The more chances they have, at informal get-togethers, at retreats, or at parties, to meet; the more they see others as human beings, the less likely it is that misunderstandings will develop. Relationships create a feeling that something worth preserving exists. When you have that, then there's a reason for making sure they work.

2. A lot of the mistakes that people make have to do with dishonesty. Students cheat and are often caught and penalized. The same is true of avaricious corporations and their leaders, corrupt politicians, plagiarizing academics and journalists, and dishonest home contractors. Ending or at least modifying such damaging behavior requires a sea change in our cultural values.

We talk a lot about ethics, but we do very little about them. It's like that old saw, "Everyone talks about the weather, but no one does anything about it." What's needed is training in ethics that begins in preschool. It is possible to develop discussions and activities for kids that inculcate such values. The book of Proverbs intones, "Train up a child in the way he should go, and even when he is old, he will not depart from it." It has a point. Such courses should be given at all levels of schooling. It's not only the teachings. It's showing our young that we care.

3. Society functions because of what Rousseau called, "The Social Contract." If everybody wanted to steal things from stores and people's homes, there aren't enough cops who could stop them. The system works because most of us *agree* that stealing is wrong. But we need rules and laws, however, for the minority who don't buy into the idea that there's right and wrong because when people see others getting away with things, they are apt to see no reason to act morally themselves. Forbidding teachers to give the same tests, adding proctors, in short, removing all temptation, can go a long way.

4. Above all, it's critical that we create positive peer pressure that looks down upon, say, cheating, that thinks it's not cool. The students will ultimately be the best advocates because it's their lives that are most directly affected. Business leaders need to develop similar guidelines and sanctions and so do government organizations of all kinds. The scientific community can greatly reduce fraud, for example, by strengthening its internal review systems and by severely punishing violators. Senior researchers should be compelled to vouch for the work of junior researchers. That way they can't blame it on their employees when they're caught. Everyone knows that physicians and pharmaceutical companies often have a too-cozy relationship, one that invites corruption. Pressure needs to be brought upon both parties to create distance

between the two. And that pressure has to come from the people, who demand reform through laws from their elected legislators.

5. Every society has icons, talented people whom we all admire. When those people take a fall because of their misdeeds it is imperative that they be dealt with severely. Why? Because everyone's watching. Thus, a Tiger Woods, a Mel Gibson, or an Eliot Spitzer needs to have the book thrown at them. We talk about role models as people to emulate. If we allow bad role models to escape punishment, then we have only ourselves to blame when lesser mortals copy what they do.

6. Most important, perhaps, we need, as Robert Putnam stresses, to reconnect. As beneficial as technology is, it has also caused us to lose much of our desire and even ability to relate to each other. When that happens, we become insensitive to the feelings and needs of others, and so miscalculations are easy to make. Renewing our commitment to community will only come about when the leaders of our economic, cultural, educational, and political institutions recognize how crucial it is for maintaining our cohesiveness as a society. And the impetus for that will come through public pressure from the people themselves.

MODERATION ABOVE ALL:
CURB YOUR APPETITE FOR POWER

1. Overconfidence is a main cause of arrogance. Such people will usually listen only to their friends and lovers. Look at what happened to Peter Chung when he went to Korea and sent back those e-mails that cost him his cushy job. When you're far away from home, there's often no one to tell you you're acting like a jerk. Remember what can and has happened to either famous people like Bill Clinton or perhaps others you know personally, if you go too far.

2. Jealousy is frequently the first step to hatred and when you display hubris, you're asking for it. Look at Bill Clinton who, when asked why he had an affair with Monica Lewinsky, quipped, "Because I could." Well, you can't, at least not usually. Stew Leonard made scads of money in his dairy business, but he too was brought low. The lesson is that the higher you go, the more people there are gunning for you. Those with power and fame need to absorb that lesson very well.

3. If you have a touch of arrogance but want to succeed, the best thing you can do is hide it. You need to pretend, convincingly, that you don't have a secret craving for power and that includes not telling people what you would do if you were in charge. Such proclamations inevitably inspire fear and dread in those who hear them. Plus, people have an almost impish wish to cut down to size those who appear to deserve it. Hold your fire until the weapons are completely within your possession.

4. Gary Hart made a classic error when he dared reporters to follow him. They did and discovered much grist for their mills. If you're guilty of something, don't push it too far. Bluffing doesn't usually work. When you challenge people you often awaken in them a desire to prove you wrong. Always be mindful of the risks you're incurring by your behavior.

5. If you're too attached to your own role as a dominant person, it can be almost impossible to enter a relationship without seeking the upper hand. But once you try it the other way, it can be liberating, even wonderful. The trick is to cultivate relationships where others affect you. Find a mentor, or an expert you respect. Take a class. Engage in team projects like house building or crew where your own contribution doesn't matter any more than another's. Most of all, seek tough criticism, the tougher the better. But, of course, you have to *want* to do it. Often, this happens when, as in Clinton's case, disastrous consequences make you wake up and pay attention.

6. Remember where you came from. One practical way of doing that is by retaining your friendships with those who knew you on the way up. These individuals are more apt to both care about you and to tell you the truths you need to hear. Spend quality time with intimates and people unconnected to your work. Include people in your circle of friends who have no stake or investment in your career. They will be great sounding boards when you need one. Avoid sycophants who will only tell you what they think you want to know.

LESS IS MORE: COUNT YOUR BLESSINGS

1. Often, we confuse what we wish would be the case with what is. Recognize what you're doing. It's because you want it so badly. But that doesn't bring you any closer to your goal. Before you do something stupid, like get on a basketball court with guys ten years younger who can really hurt you, however unintentionally, realize that playing with them doesn't make you a day younger, just more foolish. Visualize how you'll feel with a torn ligament or shoulder separation. Hopefully, you'll sit it out and stay healthy.

2. Greed may not be curable, but considering the mayhem it can bring about, trying to cure it is definitely worth a shot. Knowing when you have it good is critical. So much of the trouble people get into comes from overreaching. When its root cause is psychological, therapy should be an option, but for some, being reminded of the fates of those who, like Bernie Madoff, went too far may also be helpful.

3. If you find that you have an addiction to approval, praise, or the validation of short-term accomplishments, then you'll be gripped by a fear of living without them. Every time you seek these benchmarks, you reinforce that fear. Conversely, every time you deprive yourself, the need begins to subside. And

that's the key: start trying to live without the cushion of quick reward. When you're tempted to ask someone what she thought of your work or performance, stop for a moment. Test yourself. See how long you can go without asking for approval at all. Similarly, see how long you can talk to other people without trying to impress them. It'll be hard at first. But ultimately, it will be relaxing, even rewarding and people will like you better. What's more, you'll ultimately emerge with a stronger sense of self-esteem, instead of a shallow and artificial self-opinion.

4. The scholar and psychoanalyst Dr. Paul Marcus pushes people to heal by transcending themselves, by focusing on their responsibilities to others. He treats many people who have made some colossal blunders in pursuit of a certain self-image. It's not about what you do for others, he says. It's about others. If this book has any message, it's a clarion call for more of that. If we're less worried about who we are, then we won't need to be better, brighter, or more accomplished. We don't have to be special to do special things. And if we can resist the urge to be special at all costs, we may find ourselves acting a lot less dumb.

5. When charitable organizations look the other way at how the money they accept was acquired, they are aiding and abetting dishonesty. This is because those who give are all too often motivated by the accolades they receive for their donations and their appetite for them can be insatiable. Examples are slumlords, unethical businessmen, and those who earn their money from illegal operations like gambling and prostitution. Society needs to do its part by discouraging such behavior.

6. When reporters like *USA Today*'s Jack Kelley are lionized within their profession, it reflects greed for the big story. The same is true for medicine, law, and a host of other professions. Those in control must exercise self-restraint and be guided by an awareness that shady practices will ultimately leave their own reputations in tatters.

7. Another important consideration is to never confuse access with entitlement. Politicians are highly vulnerable to temptation because money is something they dispense. They are offered bribes and "investment opportunities." They and others in similar positions need to remember that even if the chance of apprehension is small, the loss of status is probably great enough to make it not worthwhile.

LEARN TO LISTEN: RESPECT IS A TWO-WAY STREET

1. Honor's a tough thing to deal with because it's something we really consider important. Nobody likes being "dissed" unless they're a masochist. But frequently we take it too personally. We see it as a personal assault on our dignity. The trick is to not take it personally and recognize that most of the time your honor will not be permanently affected. Someone may insult you at a party, but how many other people heard it, or even paid attention? More to the point, for how long will anyone remember it? Most people are too into what they're doing to give these things much thought. Realize that what's a big deal to you isn't to the other people because it's you and not them who was the target.

2. Mistakes with respect to honor can go in both directions. We overreact when someone challenges our sense of it, but we can also be careless about how others are likely to be affected by it. Offend the wrong person and they can shoot you. In this sense we need to role-play and think about how we'd feel if we were in their shoes. When you walk onto someone's property, it may be a person who sees their property as a literal extension of themselves. You need to always be alert to that possibility and its potential explosiveness. This is particularly likely to result in an erroneous judgment on your part if you don't share the other party's perspective.

3. Another danger zone is when you're dealing with someone who's already down and out. Because they don't have much to lose, their reaction to insults can be dangerous. That's what happened with a young middle class woman who told a group of teenagers from a poor neighborhood, "What are you going to do, shoot me?" Interpreting that as a challenge to their sense of self-respect, they did shoot her, killing her. Know that in an open society people from vastly different worlds are only an encounter away from each other. The simple credo is to respect everyone. This is particularly true when traveling in foreign countries, where the customs and values are unfamiliar to you.

4. Don't let people push you into doing something rash out of concern for your own honor. Let's say you're angry because someone asked you to leave a party. Don't go on the warpath over it. Look at the slight in perspective and decide if it's worth it. Don't decide that you're never talking to someone again because they refused to help you with something. Maybe they will next time. Weigh the costs and benefits of your actions, especially when thinking about suing over a minor issue. In such cases, the biggest beneficiaries are usually the lawyers. Think it through before you do anything.

5. Honor, and provocation, it turns out, are social phenomena. But they are also tied to your personal identity and sense of boundaries. One man's provocation is another's friendly poke. It all depends on your prior perspective. How and where do you set the borders? What do you consider to be an invasion? If you're a volcano "waiting to erupt," it's at least partly of your own making. Ask yourself if your self-identity makes you the type of person who could explode. And if so, get advice from professionals on how to prevent it from being activated.

6. Imagine if we could avoid regarding so many domains as mine or yours, so many trespasses as unjust or unfair. Or if we could avoid regarding mistreatments—being hung up on, or ignored,

or "dissed"—as encroachments on our very personhood. Well, we can't right away. But we can build up a greater tolerance for such "intrusions." After all, we choose to define our space a certain way. Buddhists, for example, deny the difference between one person and the world around him. Shunning the notion of property and boundaries, they see just one world, one universe; mounds of dirt and water and flesh and rock. We don't have to go to that extreme. But we can try not to think of a patch of road, a lane, or a call back, as our rightful property.

It starts with being freer with our immediate personal space. Let people borrow your things. Let it go if someone brushes up against you or picks up something of yours for a moment. It won't be pleasant at first, but it's a useful way to become freer of anxiety, tension, and competitive territorial feelings. It's called "systematic desensitization." We tolerate minor little intrusions, things we couldn't take before, gradually upping the ante. Let people handle your objects, even yourself—within limits. Eventually, we get a better perspective. We can train ourselves to be less territorial.

NOBODY'S PERFECT: UNDERSTAND AND APPRECIATE THAT

1. When you've lied and you feel that you're about to be exposed, don't keep it a secret from everyone. Pick someone you trust and confide in them. This will take the pressure off you and give you extra brainpower from a more objective person as you try to figure out what to do. Don't worry that they'll expose you. Most of the time, taking someone into your confidence ensures their silence because they feel honored that you trusted them and would feel extremely guilty about being shown unworthy of that trust.

2. Try not to "push the envelope." If you've done reasonably well in your life, don't try to embellish on it. This is not because you'll be found out. It's because the gain doesn't justify the risk in most cases. You worked hard to get to where you are. Why spoil it with a fib that could backfire on you? Remember that honesty is valued in many situations because it's viewed as courageous. And remember that the pleasure you'll derive from exaggerating your achievements isn't worth much because you know you're not who you say you are.

3. Resist the temptation to accept a job or anything else for which you are clearly unqualified. Chances are, you'll fall flat on your face eventually. Look at what happened to former judge Sol Wachtler when he was put on the basketball team and couldn't even catch the ball. Look at what happened to the student who got into a top-ranked college and couldn't handle the work.

4. Follow the dictum about never putting off until tomorrow what you can do today. Fix that leaky roof before it ruins your ceiling. Send that birthday gift before it's too late to matter. And see the doctor when you're supposed to, not just when you're feeling really sick. It may seem like the easy way out not to, but whatever you ignore will invariably come back to haunt you. Realize that you're now an independent adult and that if you put things off, you're only hurting yourself.

5. Even if you're famous or powerful or fabulously wealthy, don't mistake these attributes for invincibility. The greatest person can take a fall, as the many examples in this book attest to. It's precisely when your power is threatened that you need to remember its limitations. It can't always save you from disaster. Once you absorb that reality, you'll have a better chance of knowing when a tactical retreat is the winning strategy. Clinton knew that when he was an Arkansas politician. He forgot it after he became *President* Clinton. The simple solution may appear to be denial and stonewalling, but it can and will come back to bite

you if you don't know when it's time to own up to what you've done and why it was wrong.

6. The same is true when you're unable to admit a mistake. Many times we've invested so much in a decision that we're afraid to admit it was wrong. Losing face commonly has a lot to do with it. Recognize that not acknowledging your error has *absolutely nothing* to do with the fact that you made one. In fact, it's just another error that compounds the problem. Decide in your mind what you want more—to correct the goof, or not to, and live with the consequences. If it's the latter, then move on and forget about it.

ENOUGH GUILT: GIVE YOURSELF A BREAK

1. If you're feeling insecure, and God knows, we all do at times, the first thing is to take a step back and try to figure out what's really bothering you. Is it the casual criticism about how you look that stirs a distant memory of when you were a gangly teenager? Is it the fact that you were not asked to say a few words at a party honoring an old classmate? Or might it be the laughing comments someone made about your moves as you walked off the dance floor? These are the kinds of things that can put you in a bad mood and cause you to speak harshly to those around you. Always be conscious of what's causing you to say or do things that are out of character. Knowing what's behind them will give you perspective and exert a calming influence. The same is true of stress. Know it for what it is.

2. People will say, "You can fool others, but you can't fool yourself." Admit to yourself that you care about what others think. There's nothing wrong with it. Once you do that, you won't have to feel bad about keeping your mouth shut when you re-

ally want to tell someone off. You won't have to feel resentful about having told someone a white lie about how great their cooking is. It's when, trying to assert our independence, we declare that we don't care what others think and then try to prove it by doing something ill considered that we find ourselves in trouble.

3. Bragging about one's accomplishments, as opposed to being proud of them, is a sign of insecurity. Often, people are not aware of how they sound when they do it. If they were, they'd be embarrassed. The best way to realize how it comes across to people and to stop doing it is to listen to what others sound like when *they* do it. That way you can avoid the social cost of being labeled a conceited person and suffering rejection.

4. Understand the role that guilt plays in people's lives. It's major and you can't avoid it. Whatever you do, you always wonder if it's enough. You must make every effort to become conscious of your feelings of guilt. And if you know that guilt is what's motivating you, then you'll understand when it haunts you.

5. Insecurity can make you afraid of change. We keep fixing our outdated computer because we like it, even though purchasing a new one would be cheaper and more efficient. We drive our old car that keeps breaking down because we're attached to it. We wear that old moth-eaten sweater, even though it looks terrible, and so on and so forth. We do all these things because they have significant meaning for us. If it makes you feel better that's fine, but recognize why you're doing it.

DON'T LET EMOTIONS SABOTAGE YOU

1. A key element here is not to allow our personal prejudices to get in the way of our decisions. When Harry Frazee allowed Babe

Ruth to get away from the Red Sox, his personal dislike of the man had a great deal to do with it. You need to step back and ask yourself why you really oppose something. And then ask yourself if that dislike is more important than the success of your project or your company, or whatever it is you're trying to obtain.

2. Emotions are a major impediment to making the right choice. We hate, we love, we're angry, sad, depressed, the whole gamut. And when these powerful feelings come into play, it mightily affects decision-making. Once you recognize their role, you can address the problem. And one solution is to simply put off making a decision about anything when you're in that frame of mind. Resist the impulse to use the issue at hand as a way of relieving your emotional distress because, invariably, once the dust settles, you'll realize and regret what you did. You'll tell everyone, "I acted in the heat of the moment," but it will probably be too late to make up for it. Just tell yourself, almost dogmatically, "I'm not doing *anything* until I calm down." And you will, gradually. In truth, the old refrain "count to ten," isn't a bad idea. Why doesn't it always work? Because people are usually so mad, they forget to, or they don't even *want* to, count to ten. They'd rather enjoy their righteous anger.

3. Accept that which cannot be changed. Certain things are simply beyond our control. It's not always what happens to people that's so bad. It's how they deal with it. And the latter is more in their control. Understand that when you lash out because you're frustrated at your lack of control over something or someone, you're only creating new problems. One solution is to consider what you can do about the dilemma and what you can't. In such cases, writing it down or talking it out with someone in terms of realistic options can be of real help.

4. When something bothers you, it's good to talk about it, but the challenge is to know when to *stop* doing so. Know that as long as it's unresolved, reviewing it is just going to fuel your anger all

over again. That's because without solving the source of it, the anger has nowhere to go.

BE STRONG: GET HELP WHEN YOU NEED IT

1. If you think you might have a clinical psychological disorder, like manic-depressive illness or obsessive-compulsive disorder, go for help. Ditto for any substance abuse problems. Don't be a hero because you're too *macho* to acknowledge the possibility. It's not a sign of weakness to go for help; it's a sign of weakness *not to*. I had a student at City College who came to me after the Virginia Tech murders and said he was afraid he was going to either harm himself or others. A native of Thailand and a practicing Buddhist, he nevertheless felt that when people saw him on the subway with his backpack they would "stare at me as if I were a Muslim terrorist." I arranged for him to go to the college counseling center and he rapidly improved.

2. People sometimes get a little paranoid. It usually happens when they're already feeling insecure. You know you feel it when you think everyone's against you but realize that it's an exaggeration. It usually comes to the surface after you've had negative experiences with a couple of people, one after another. We all have days like that, days when we wish we'd stayed in bed. The airline reservations clerk is nasty to you, your boss yells at you, and a restaurant takes forever to seat you. The best thing you can do is to get a reality check. Ask someone you trust if they think you're being paranoid or if there's a rational explanation for all these events. It's particularly useful when you're worried that someone has something against you. Carefully explain your reasons for thinking it to your soul mate or whomever and see how it sounds to you and to him or her. But whatever you do, don't keep it bottled up inside.

SOME FINAL THOUGHTS

The dumb things we do affect the quality of our lives. They often leave us feeling angry, depressed, and frustrated. We wonder how we got into this or that predicament and why things can't be better. We spend so much time trying to fix things, trying to get people to do our bidding and, ultimately, feeling bad about what we did and about what others did to us.

A book is not a panacea for rash and foolish behavior. It's not going to end it, but it can, perhaps, reduce it significantly by providing insight, perspective, and concrete ideas and solutions. When things happen that we don't like, we need to first stop and gather our thoughts before we act. To do so effectively requires that we be in the right frame of mind and if we're not, we should wait until we are. We also need to discuss our options with other people whom we trust. When we act, we need to be sensitive to how others might respond or not respond to what we do. Having done all that, we still have to accept that we might not get the result we want, but at least we've given it our best effort.

****

I'd like to conclude with a request of you, the reader. The stories in this book are just a few of the millions of examples that demonstrate the folly humans are capable of. I'm sure each of you has a story or two to tell that would be of value to others. Perhaps it might help them avoid making a similar mistake.

In that spirit I'd like to invite you to do just that. If there's a dumb thing that you've done or know about, please feel free to share it with me. And if you have a good idea as to why it happened I'd love to know that too. You can contact me on my website whatwasIthinking?.com

"Only two things are infinite, the universe and human stupidity, and I'm not sure about the former."

—Albert Einstein

References

Adut, Ari. 2008. *On Scandal: Moral Disturbances in Society, Politics, and Art.* Cambridge: Cambridge University Press.

Amato, P. R., and Alan Booth. 1997. *A Generation at Risk: Growing Up in an Era of Family Upheaval.* Cambridge, MA: Harvard University Press.

Araton, Harvey. 2008. "A Day to 'Misremember': Politicians Turn Hearing Into a Partisan Squabble." *New York Times*, February 14, D1.

Babel. 2006. Directed by Alejandro Gonzalez Inarritu. Brad Pitt, Cate Blanchett. Hollywood, CA: Paramount.

Barboza, David. 2006. "In a Computer Scientist's Fall, China Feels Robbed of Glory." *New York Times*, May 15, A1.

Begley, Sharon. 2006. "You Might Help a Teen Avoid Dumb Behavior by Nurturing Intuition." *Wall Street Journal*, November 3, B1.

Blood and Tears. 2007. Directed by Isidore Rosmarin, Jeff Helmreich, associate director. New York: ThinkFilm

Blumenthal, Ralph, and Sarah Lyall. 1999. "Repeat Accusations of Plagiarism Taint Prolific Biographer." *New York Times*, September 21, A1.

Bumiller, Elizabeth. 2004. "Missteps Cited in Kerik Vetting by White House." *New York Times*, December 15, A1.

Caher, John M. 1998. *King of the Mountain: The Rise, Fall, and Redemption of Chief Judge Sol Wachtler.* Amherst, NY: Prometheus Books.

Carey, Benedict. 2008. "Feel Like a Fraud? At Times, Maybe you Should." *New York Times*, February 5, F1.

———. 2010. "Why All Indiscretions Appear Youthful." *New York Times*, October 5: D1.

Clinton, Bill. 2002. *My Life.* New York: Alfred A. Knopf.

Comisky, Ian, Lawrence Feld, and Steven Harris. 1995. *Tax Fraud and Evasion* (vols. 1 and 2). New York: Research Institute of America.

Conniff, Richard. 2007. "The Rich are More Oblivious Than You and Me." *New York Times*, Op-Ed page, April 4, A15.

Cowan, Alison Leigh. 2008. "Death of Troubled Connecticut Surgeon Leads to Charges Against an Employee." *New York Times*, January 26, B2.

Crazy Love. 2007. Directed by Dan Klores and Fisher Stevens. New York: Magnolia Films.

Cupchik, Will. 2002. *Why Honest People Shoplift or Commit Other Acts of Theft*. Toronto: Tagami Communications.

Dana, Jason, and George Loewenstein. 2003. "A Social Science Perspective on Gifts to Physicians From Industry." *Journal of the American Medical Association*. 290 (2), 252–55.

Dreifus, Claudia. 2007. "Finding Hope in Knowing the Universal Capacity for Evil." *New York Times*, April 3, F2.

Fass, Mark. 2004. "CITYPEOPLE: A Sort of Love Story." *New York Times,* March 21.

Firebaugh, Glenn, and Laura Tach. 2005. "Relative Income and Happiness: Are Americans on a Hedonic Treadmill?" Paper presented at the Annual Meeting of the American Sociological Association.

Fishman, Steve. 2010. "Bernie Madoff, Free at Last." *New York Magazine*, June 7.

Foderaro, Lisa W., and Jennifer Medina. 2006. "Downfall of a Young and Ambitious Assemblyman Stuns His Constituents." *New York Times*, May 27, B4.

Freud, Sigmund. 1960. *The Psychopathology of Everyday Life*. New York: W. W. Norton, 1960. Translated by Alan Tyson and edited by James Strachey.

Gabriel, Trip. 2010. "Plagiarism Lines Blur for Students in Digital Age." *New York Times*, August 2: A1.

Gladwell, Malcolm. 2005. *Blink: The Power of Thinking Without Thinking*. New York: Little, Brown and Company.

Glanville, Doug. 2008. "In Baseball, Fear Bats At the Top of the Order." *New York Times*, January 16, A23.

Goffman, Erving. 2007. *Asylums*. New Brunswick, NJ: Transaction Books.

Goleman, Daniel. 1995. *Emotional Intelligence*. New York: Bantam.

———. 2006. *Social Intelligence: The New Science of Human Relationships*. New York: Bantam.

Harmon, Amy. 2006. "That Wild Streak? Maybe it Runs in the Family." *New York Times*, June 15, A1.

Hastings, Michael. 2010. "The Runaway General." *Rolling Stone*, June 22, 90.

Healy, Patrick. 2003. "L. I. Suspect Pleads Not Guilty in a Fatal Traffic Stabbing." *New York Times*, June 20, B8.

Helmreich, William B. 1982, 1984. *The Things They Say Behind Your Back: Stereotypes and the Myths Behind Them*. New York: Doubleday, New Brunswick, NJ: Transaction Books.

Hernandez, Raymond. 2010. "Candidate's Words Differ From History." *New York Times*, May 8, A1.

Hick, Jonathan, B. 2006. "Candidate for Congress in Brooklyn Admits Her College Credits Fell Short." *New York Times*, August 24, B5.

Horowitz, Adam, and Business 2.0. 2004. *The Dumbest Moments in Business History*. New York: Portfolio/Penguin.

Interlandi, Jeneen. 2006. "An Unwelcome Discovery." *New York Times Magazine*, October 22, 98–103.

Itzkoff, Dave. 2007. "A One-Way Ticket to Disaster." *New York Times*, Sunday Styles, December 30: 1.

Jones, Marilee, and Kenneth R. Ginsburg. 2006. *Less Stress, More Success: A New Approach to Guiding Your Teens Through College Admissions and Beyond*. American Academy of Pediatrics.

Katz, Jack. 1988. *Seductions of Crime: Moral and Sensual Attractions in Doing Evil*. New York: Basic Books.

Katz, James E., and Ronald E. Rice. 2002. *Social Consequences of Internet Use: Access, Involvement, and Interaction*. Cambridge, MA: MIT Press.

Khaneman, Daniel, and Amos Tversky, eds. 2000. *Choices, Values, and Frames*. New York: Cambridge University Press & Russell Sage Foundation.

Kilgannon, Corey. 2007. "Defendant's Son on Stand In Killing of L.I. Teenager." *New York Times*, December 11, B5.

Kipnis, Laura. 2010. *How to Become a Scandal*. New York: Metropolitan Books.

Kirtzman, Andrew. 2009. *Betrayal: The Life and Lies of Bernie Madoff*. New York: HarperCollins.

Krull, D.S., and C.A. Anderson. "The Process of Explanation." *Current Directions in Psychological Science*, 6: 1–5.

Lee, Felicia. 2003. "Are More People Cheating?" *New York Times*, October 4, B7.

Leonard, Nancy H., and Michael Harvey. 2007. "Negative Perfectionism: Examining Negative Excessive Behavior in the Workplace." *Journal of Applied Social Psychology* 38 (3): 585–610.

Lewin, Tamar. 2007. "M.I.T.'s Admissions Dean Resigns: Ends 28-Year Lie About Degrees." *New York Times*, April 28, A1.

Luhmann, Niklas. 2002. *Risk: A Sociological Theory*. New Brunswick, NJ: Transaction Books.

Marcus, Paul. 2003. *Ancient Religious Wisdom, Spirituality, and Psychoanalysis.* Westport, CT: Praeger.

———. 2008. *Being for the Other: Emmanuel Levinas, Ethical Living, and Psychoanalysis.* Milwaukee, WI: Marquette University Press.

———. 2010. *In Search of the Good Life: Emmanuel Levinas, Psychoanalysis and the Art of Living.* London: Karnac Books.

Marin, Rick. 2001. "Is This the Face of a Midlife Crisis?" *New York Times,* June 24, section 9:1.

McCord, William, and Joan McCord. 1964. *The Psychopath.* New York: Van Nostrand-Reinhold.

Newman, Katherine S., et al. 2004. *Rampage: The Social Roots of School Shootings.* New York: Basic Books.

Padgett, Tim. 2009. "Sanford's Sex Scandal: Assessing the Damage." *TIME,* June 25.

Post, Jerrold M. 2004. *Leaders and Their Followers in a Dangerous World: The Psychology of Political Behavior.* Ithaca, NY: Cornell University Press.

Powell, Michael, and Russ Buetnner. 2008. "The Long Run: In Matters Big and Small, Crossing Giuliani Had Price." *New York Times,* January 22, A1.

Preston, Jennifer. 1990. *Queen Bess: An Unauthorized Biography of Bess Myerson.* Chicago: Contemporary Books.

Putnam, Robert D. 2000. *Bowling Alone: The Collapse and Revival of American Community.* New York: Simon & Schuster.

Rayner, Steven. 2010. "Channelling Ike." *New Yorker,* April 26.

Resurrecting the Champ. 2006. Directed by Rod Lurie. Starring Samuel Jackson and Josh Hartnett. Los Angeles, CA: Yari Film Group.

Riding, Alan. 2007. "Pianist's Widower Admits Fraud in Recordings Issued as his Wife's." *New York Times,* February 27, B3.

Robbins, Alexandra, and Abby Wilner. 2001. *Quarterlife Crisis: The Unique Challenges of Life in Your Twenties.* New York: Penguin.

Schwartz, John. 2007. "From Spaceflight to Attempted Murder Charge." *New York Times,* February 7, A1.

Smith, Emily, Jeane MacIntosh, David K. Li, and Kate Sheehy. 2009. "All Over Me." *New York Post,* December 2, 5.

Smothers, Ronald. 1997. "In a Passion for Antique Clocks, Executive Embezzled $12 Million." *New York Times,* October 1.

Steinberg, Jacques. 2004. "Writer's Work in USA Today is Called False." *The New York Times,* March 20, A1.

Sternberg, Robert J. ed. 2002. *Why Smart People Can be So Stupid.* New Haven, CT: Yale University Press.

Thomas, Landon Jr. 2008. "What's $34 Billion on Wall St.? A Subprime Strategy Implodes. But Some of its Captains Are Just Fine." *New York Times,* January 27, Sunday Business Section, 1.

Toobin, Jeffrey. 1999. *A Vast Conspiracy: The Real Story of the Sex Scandal that Nearly Brought Down a President.* New York: Random House.

Volkan, Vamik. 2004. *Blind Trust: Large Groups and their Leaders in Times of Crisis and Terror.* Charlottesville, VA: Pitchstone Publishing.

Wachtler, Sol. 1997. *After the Madness.* New York: Random House.

Wegner, Daniel M. 2009. "How to Think, Say, or Do Precisely the Worst Thing For Any Occasion." *Science* 325: 48–51.

Whitehead, Barbara Dafoe, and David Popenoe. 2001. "Who Wants to Marry a Soul Mate? New Survey Findings on Young Adults' Attitudes about Love and Marriage." In *The State of Our Unions, 2001: The Social Health of Marriage in America.* New Brunswick, NJ: The National Marriage Project.

Wolfe, Linda. 1994. *Double Life: The Shattering Affair Between Chief Judge Sol Wachtler and Socialite Joy Silverman.* New York: Simon & Schuster.

Wolfe, Tom. 1987. *The Bonfire of the Vanities.* New York: Farrar, Straus, & Giroux.

Zernicke, Kate, and Abby Goodnough. 2006. "Lawmaker Quits Over E-Mail Sent to Teenage Pages." *New York Times,* September 30, A1.

Zimbardo, Philip. 2007. *The Lucifer Effect: Understanding How Good People Turn Evil.* New York: Random House.

index

about the Author

William B. Helmreich is professor of sociology at City University Graduate Center and City College of New York where he serves as Deputy Chairman. He has also taught at Yale University and is a former Woodrow Wilson Fellow. Dr. Helmreich is the author of ten books, including *The Things They Say Behind Your Back*; *Flight Path: How to Get the Job That Launches Your Career After College* with Neil Kalt; *Against All Odds*; and *The Black Crusaders*. In addition, he has edited three volumes, including the textbook, *Contemporary Issues in Society* with Hugh Lena and William McCord. Helmreich has also written for the *New York Times*, *Newsday*, and the *Los Angeles Times*. He has been interviewed by Oprah and Larry King and was a guest anchor on *NBC TV News*.

Dr. Helmreich's latest book project, tentatively titled *Walking 3,000 Miles in New York City: A Sociologist's Journey*, concerns how New York City has changed in the last thirty-five years. In addition, he received a $285,000 grant from the U.S. Department of Education to establish the Center for Ethnic & Racial Understanding at Queens College. Its purpose is to find new ways to resolve conflict between members of various groups who strongly dislike each other. He resides in New York with his wife and three children.